At Issue

Does Outsourcing Harm America?

Other books in the At Issue series:

At Issue

Does Outsourcing Harm America?

Katherine Read Dunbar, Book Editor

GREENHAVEN PRESS

An imprint of Thomson Gale, a part of The Thomson Corporation

Detroit • New York • San Francisco • San Diego • New Haven, Conn.
Waterville, Maine • London • Munich

Bonnie Szumski, *Publisher*
Helen Cothran, *Managing Editor*

© 2006 Thomson Gale, a part of The Thomson Corporation.

Thomson and Star Logo are trademarks and Gale and Greenhaven Press are registered trademarks used herein under license.

For more information, contact:
Greenhaven Press
27500 Drake Rd.
Farmington Hills, MI 48331-3535
Or you can visit our Internet site at http://www.gale.com

Articles in Greenhaven Press anthologies are often edited for length to meet page requirements. In addition, original titles of these works are changed to clearly present the main thesis and to explicitly indicate the author's opinion. Every effort is made to ensure that Greenhaven Press accurately reflects the original intent of the authors. Every effort has been made to trace the owners of copyrighted material.

Cover photographs reproduced by permission of GStar/PhotoDisc.

LIBRARY OF CONGRESS CATALOGING-IN-PUBLICATION DATA

Does Outsourcing Harm America? / Katherine Read Dunbar, book editor.
p. cm. -- (At issue)
Includes bibliographical references and index.
0-7377-3391-8 (lib. : alk. paper) 0-7377-3392-6 (pbk. : alk. paper)
1. Contracting out--United States. 2. Labor Market--United States.
3. Personnel management--United States. 4. United States--Economic conditions. I. Dunbar, Katherine Read. II. At issue (San Diego, Calif.)
HD2365.D64 2006
330.973--dc22
                                                        2006041174

Printed in the United States of America
10 9 8 7 6 5 4 3 2 1

Contents

Introduction

Outsourcing is a business practice in which a company hires service providers, usually located outside of the country, to do work that the company believes can be performed more efficiently and less expensively by these outside contractors. With the advent of the Internet and high-speed networks spanning the globe, more jobs than ever before can easily be transferred to other countries. In an age of globalization, the location of workers performing many jobs has become largely irrelevant. However, the practice of outsourcing has become the source of heated debate in the United States. Many people blame much of the country's unemployment on outsourcing and are alarmed by predictions that millions more jobs will be outsourced in the coming years. To better understand the current debate over outsourcing, it is important to know a little about the history of the practice, the kinds of jobs that are being outsourced, and the countries to which jobs are being transferred.

Outsourcing is a much older practice than some people realize. In colonial days, American businesses outsourced the production of covered-wagon covers and clipper ships' sails to workers in Scotland. The raw material for these products was imported from India. A couple of hundred years later, in the 1970s, computer companies began to outsource their payroll applications to outside service providers. However, most of these jobs were outsourced to companies in other states rather than overseas. It was in the late 1980s that the practice of outsourcing began to boom. During this time the field of information technology (IT) was growing rapidly, and the demand for IT workers who could develop hardware and software exploded. As the Internet and telecommunications fields developed, companies created thousands of high-paying jobs to attract talented IT employees to work for them. As the U.S.

economy faltered, however, companies had to cut their IT budgets and began to seek a less expensive labor force outside of the United States.

India, with its large population of English speakers and trained workers, was one of the first countries to benefit from the outsourcing trend. Americans companies began outsourcing some of their low-end IT jobs to India in the early 1990s and have gradually outsourced a wide variety of work, including call center servicing, medical transcription, tax return preparation, research and development, and medical data analysis. Cities like Bangalore have become well known for their skylines dotted with call center buildings that seem to have cropped up overnight. Providing customer service to American consumers for American companies, call center workers are highly educated and earn what are considered top-tier salaries in India. However, these salaries are still far lower than those commanded for the same jobs in the United States. Many Americans, particularly those who have lost their jobs to outsourcing, are frustrated about having to compete for their jobs with workers in foreign countries who are able to work for far less money.

Since the 1990s American companies have expanded beyond India and are outsourcing jobs to many other countries, including China, Canada, Argentina, and the Philippines. As CNN political analyst Carlos Watson notes, although the media focuses on the many jobs being outsourced to India, three to four times as many jobs have actually been outsourced to China in the last fifteen years, mainly in the manufacturing field. John C. McCarthy, an analyst for market-research company Forrester Research Inc., has predicted that by 2015 U.S. businesses will outsource at least 3.3 million white-collar jobs to India, China, Russia, Pakistan, and Vietnam. In addition, many jobs are being outsourced to Europe, particularly to Eastern European countries. In fact, the Global Envision organization estimates that soon 25 percent of total global expenditures on outsourcing will go to Europe.

Outsourcing has thus become an important trend in business strategy, with many companies claiming that having offshore capabilities is crucial for competitiveness in the global marketplace. American corporations also assert that outsourcing leads to increased efficiency because it allows companies to focus on their own strengths, channeling their resources into areas in which they excel and utilizing outside labor for areas in which they are less strong. Not only does outsourcing contribute to efficiency, it is also a major source of cost-savings. Sudhakar Shenoy, chairman and chief executive officer of a Reston consulting firm, argues that the cost-savings from outsourcing are huge. Remarking on a recent project in which she advised clients to outsource, Shenoy said, "In the end, the job was done in India for less than $400,000. The same job in the U.S. would've cost more than $3 million."

Although proponents of outsourcing claim that the numbers speak for themselves, critics assert that corporations fail to consider the additional costs of operating overseas when calculating how much savings outsourcing brings. According to Hank Zupnick, chief information officer of GE Real Estate, when hidden costs are considered, "someone in India working for $10,000 a year can actually end up costing the company four to eight times that amount." While outsourcing may look cheaper on the surface, some experts argue that the costs associated with setting up, operating, and maintaining quality thousands of miles away often outweigh the benefits.

Opponents of outsourcing are also concerned about the hundreds of thousands of Americans losing jobs to outsourcing. Increasingly, these displaced workers are highly educated people with advanced degrees in fields including engineering, radiology, mathematics, and information technology. They are being replaced by equally well-educated but lower-salaried workers in India and China. Although some economists argue that more education and retraining is the solution for workers displaced by outsourcing, others argue that people who have already spent years studying one field will have little motivation to retrain in another field since their jobs in the new field may also be outsourced in the future. These displaced employees may never be able to find the same quality jobs that are lost to outsourcing.

A growing sentiment among Americans that they are losing their jobs to foreign workers has spurred many to demand protection from the government. In 2005 nearly all fifty U.S. states proposed legislation that would either prohibit or severely limit outsourcing. Some business leaders, such as Carly Fiorina, chairman of computing and software company Hewlett-Packard, strenuously argue against this protectionist approach, asserting that it will be harmful to American companies. Fiorina states, "We must do what Americans have always done—work to keep our country in the lead, by making it the most competitive and creative of all nations."

With concerns about lost jobs and outsourcing's effect on the economy, this issue is extremely important to many people and is hotly debated. Critics predict that outsourcing will lead to America's economic and ultimately global decline, but others, including U.S. chief economic advisor Gregory Mankiw, see outsourcing as simply "a new way of doing international trade." In *At Issue: Does Outsourcing Harm America?* the authors offer various views on the debate over whether outsourcing is harmful to the United States.

1

Outsourcing Harms America

Lou Dobbs

Lou Dobbs is a nationally syndicated columnist and is the anchor and managing editor for CNN's program Lou Dobbs Tonight.

Despite evidence that outsourcing is actually hurting America, Gregory Mankiw, chairman of the President's Council of Economic Advisers has labeled outsourcing as a new way of doing international trade, asserting that it is good for the economy. In addition, large multinational corporations and the George W. Bush administration vigorously defend outsourcing, claiming that it is necessary for the country to remain competitive. Unfortunately, such claims are not supported by concrete evidence and fail to take into account the damage that outsourcing is causing in America in the form of technology and job losses and an enormous trade deficit.

Gregory Mankiw is a lanky, bespectacled, low-key guy who looks the part of a former Harvard professor of economics, which he is. Mankiw has written a number of popular economics textbooks. He's also the chairman of the President's Council of Economic Advisers, and along with the president's economics adviser, Stephen Friedman, he has the greatest access to President [George W.] Bush on economic policy. Mankiw, however, chose early this year [2004] to publicly support the shipment of American jobs to cheap overseas labor markets. He caused a brief outcry in Congress, and even the al-

Lou Dobbs, *Exporting America: Why Corporate Greed Is Shipping American Jobs Overseas*. New York: Warner Books, 2004. Copyright © 2004 by The Dobbs Group. Reproduced by permission of the publisher.

ways loyal Speaker of the House, Congressman Dennis Hastert, was moved to separate himself from Mankiw's statement. Mankiw said, "Outsourcing is just a new way of doing international trade. We are very used to goods being produced abroad and being shipped here on ships or planes. What we're not used to is services being produced abroad and being sent here over the Internet or telephone wires. . . . I think outsourcing is a growing phenomenon, but it's something that we should realize is probably a plus for the economy in the long run."

The Government Should Side with Working Americans

A number of people on Capitol Hill thought Mankiw should have resigned, but I disagreed. On my broadcast that night, I called on the president to fire him. Not merely because I obviously disagree with him, but because Mankiw's statement raised the administration's support of overseas outsourcing to a declaration of government policy. Now, maybe I'm being somewhat brittle about the matter, but I just happen to believe that our government should be on the side of American working men and women, not aiding and abetting the destruction of their jobs by supporting a business practice that even Mankiw said could "probably be a plus for the economy in the long run." Probably? It could also be a probable negative. It certainly is if you're one of the hundreds of thousands who've lost their jobs to outsourcing. When he added a further qualifier to his support by saying "in the long run," Mankiw kept his credentials as an economist in good standing. How long is the long run? How many jobs do we have to lose to outsourcing to determine whether it really is a "plus," or a definite negative? I invited Gregory Mankiw to join me on my show that night and a number of times since, to ask him those questions and to debate the issue, but he has consistently declined. The invitation is permanently open.

Mankiw spoke for the administration in his early support of outsourcing, and since then the Bush economic team has taken its advocacy of free trade at any price to new heights. The White House is not only making statements like "outsourcing is good for the American worker" but is defending its free trade policies by insisting that all of us who are concerned about chronic, bulging trade deficits and the outsourcing of American jobs are "economic isolationists." Really? I certainly have never called for protectionist trade policies, only fair trade polices. I've never called for an isolationist trade policy, only balanced trade. And frankly, I don't know anyone who has advocated any policy that could be honestly described as economic isolationism. And neither does the Bush administration. At a time when we should be having an honest, open dialogue about the impact of overseas outsourcing and free trade on American workers, the administration has chosen to indulge in rhetorical gamesmanship while ignoring the national cost of a half-trillion-dollar trade deficit, the huge quantities of foreign capital that we are now dependent on, and the emergence of a national policy that puts our working men and women in direct competition for employment with a third world labor force that will work far cheaper than Americans. There are a lot of misconceptions to address when we finally do begin that dialogue, and a lot of myths to dispel.

How do you tell radiologists, lawyers, or architects that they can be retrained for better careers when they've already been to college?

Myth No. 1: Outsourcing American Jobs Is Good for Our Economy

Even the chairman of the President's Council of Economic Advisers couldn't go beyond saying outsourcing is "probably" a plus for our economy, "in the long run." The problem is, there's no empirical evidence to support that position. We do know that workers who have lost their jobs to overseas outsourcing are finding new jobs that pay only about 80 percent of their original wages. And we do know that there are tremendous costs to the government to provide unemployment benefits and retrain these laid-off workers. Outsourcing may be good for the profits of U.S. multinationals, but that isn't really the issue, is it?

Myth No. 2: Outsourcing Has Improved Productivity Growth and the Creation of High-Value Jobs

Our gains in productivity have resulted from (1) improvements in business processes and operations as a result of the application of new technology, (2) employees who are lucky enough to have had jobs for the past several years and are working longer hours for basically static compensation, and (3) moving production and shipping American jobs overseas to provide goods and services to the U.S. market.

As for creation of high-value jobs, the numbers speak for themselves, and they are not encouraging. When the Bureau of Labor Statistics [BLS] released its ten-year projections for American job growth in February 2004, seven of the ten biggest areas of job growth were in menial or low-paying service jobs. Here's the BLS projection:

1. Waiters and waitresses

2. Janitors and cleaners

3. Food preparation

4. Nursing aides, orderlies, and attendants

5. Cashiers

6. Customer service representatives

7. Retail salespersons

8. Registered nurses

9. General and operational managers

10. Postsecondary teachers

Only three of these job categories require a college degree. The rest rely on on-the-job training. These jobs of the future hardly qualify as high value.

Myth No. 3: Outsourcing Is Simply a Part of Free Trade

[Economist] Adam Smith believed that free trade allowed countries to concentrate their production on goods in which they had a natural advantage, and to acquire through trade other goods better produced by other countries. [Economist] David Ricardo developed the concept of comparative advantage, which held that nations can benefit from free trade by concentrating their production on goods they can produce most efficiently, acquiring through trade other goods that permit them to concentrate on their comparative advantage and thereby enlarge their economy.

Americans are losing jobs because we permit U.S. multinationals to force American workers to compete with cheap foreign labor.

Smith and Ricardo did not envision a trade relationship in which there wasn't mutuality of benefit, that is, balance. Both economists assumed that national economies would act with a clear understanding of national self-interest. I strongly doubt that either Smith or Ricardo would be pleased to find their free trade theories being used to support the transfer of factors of production from developed nations to third world nations, to take advantage of all but limitless supplies of cheap foreign labor. They also could not have imagined that one nation would effectively risk bankrupting itself by transferring its comparative advantage of knowledge base, expertise, and capital to its trading partners, and then ship its jobs overseas as well. Our current trade policies aren't laissez-faire but rather "c'est la vie."

Myth No. 4: Our Economy and Consumers Are Strong Enough to Run Large Chronic Deficits

This bizarre assertion was made by Congressman David Dreier—one of many he's made in trying to defend free trade agreements on my show. The dapper Republican congressman from California is the personification of the free-trade-at-any-cost philosophy, and unlike many in the Republican party, he has the courage of his convictions. The congressman is partially correct, to the extent that a trade surplus might occur when an economy weakens or goes into recession, and the purchase of imports declines. But the reality is that with our chronic trade deficits we are approaching $4 trillion in accumulated trade debt and must borrow foreign capital to buy foreign goods. As a result, our massive chronic trade deficits are clear evidence that our economy is not producing enough goods for domestic consumption and not producing enough goods that the world wants to buy or can afford. If that's not weakness, I don't know what is.

Myth No. 5: The Only Alternative to Free Trade Is Protectionism

The free traders, within and without the Bush administration, have taken to casting the outsourcing and free trade arguments in terms of false choices: insisting that there is only free trade, as currently practiced, or no trade. But between the polar extremes of free trade and isolationism are a wide range of policy choices: In the center of the policy spectrum there is balanced trade. But Washington and Corporate America are opposed to balanced trade because it would mean a new direction in policy, a larger and more active role for our government, and an end to carte blanche for corporations in international trade. The real alternative to what we continue to permit Washington and Corporate America to call "free trade" is balanced trade, in which we negotiate trade agreements that are reciprocal in benefit—unlike the World Trade Organization [WTO] or trade agreements like NAFTA [North American Free Trade Agreement]. We have ten years' experience with the WTO, and we have eleven years experience with NAFTA. That experience shows that free trade is not working for the United States. When one side—namely, the United States—is carrying a half-trillion-dollar trade deficit, it's clearly not benefiting us. Many of our biggest trading partners, notably China, are engaging in obstructed trade, yet our leaders keep insisting that it's free and fair. They state that this is the only way it can work, or else we become protectionist.

Well, the Chinese are protectionists, the Japanese are, and so is much of the EU [European Union]. And they all have trade surpluses. Why should the United States not be able to achieve a surplus as well, or at least balanced trade?

Myth No. 6: Job Retraining Is the Way to Deal with Outsourcing

I think James Glassman, columnist for the *Washington Post* and an American Enterprise Institute fellow, answered this one just fine on my show. When I asked him what we would be retraining workers for, Glassman said, "One of the things about a dynamic economy is, we don't know what the jobs are." And that's the point. When you're exporting jobs that are at or near the top of what we consider professional careers, where is the next step up? How do you tell radiologists, lawyers, or architects that they can be retrained for better careers when they've already been to college, apprenticed, and interned and now are in desirable and well-paying positions? What are they going to be offered in the way of a better job?

When free traders like Glassman say, "Don't worry, we retrained blacksmiths after the advent of automobiles," they're talking about a move from one kind of production to a new one. We didn't just stop using horses and wait around for a better form of transportation—it had already arrived. That, however, is what's happening with outsourcing of American jobs. We're outsourcing high-paying service and professional jobs, yet there isn't a new job that is attracting labor, at least not in this country. Blacksmiths didn't lose their livelihood and then wait years for the introduction of the automobile. The automobile industry that forced blacksmiths and carriage makers out of business simultaneously created new jobs. Americans are not losing their jobs to a dynamic, rapidly changing economy. Americans are losing jobs because we permit U.S. multinationals to force American workers to compete with cheap foreign labor.

Myth No. 7: Outsourcing Benefits Everyone

"Insourcing," as the Bush administration, the multinationals, and other free traders like to call the building of foreign factories in this country, is a sham argument. Honda, Toyota, and BMW, for example, built plants here to win access to the world's richest car markets. That required them to make an investment in American-based facilities and American workers. There is no similarity of any kind between the foreign companies' hiring of Americans to staff these "transplants" and the exporting of American jobs to India or other third world countries simply to take advantage of cheap labor, rather than enter a foreign market. The hiring of American workers in plants owned by foreign companies is not analogous in any way to IBM's shipping 10,000 jobs to India solely for the purpose of paying lower wages.

As I've mentioned, under the direction of the Reagan Administration, the U.S. Congress and U.S. trade representative forced import quotas against Japanese auto manufacturers after Japanese vehicle exports swamped our shores. The administration forced the building of plants by companies like Honda and Nissan and BMW in return for greater access to the world's largest consumer market. What the current administration and free trade proponents like to call "insourcing" is really just foreign direct investment in the United States.

Those foreign-based companies build here, and they sell here. They don't build cars here and then send those cars back to Japan or Germany for sale. They are building here to get access to our market, and they're doing a good job of it. On the other hand, our trade agreements rarely open up foreign markets to the degree that the United States has opened up its markets. We don't sell into those other markets, because we can't.

Myth No. 8: The Goal of Outsourcing Jobs Overseas Is to Increase Productivity

Outsourcing proponents claim that it's all about productivity, not price. Almost everyone agrees that the American worker is the most highly productive worker in the world—and among the costliest. But for reasons of public relations, U.S. multinationals are loath to say they're exporting American jobs simply to cut their labor costs. No, instead they or their consultants say they're shipping jobs to cheap foreign labor markets to achieve "efficiency" or "higher productivity" or to raise their competitiveness. Nonsense. It's like the old saying: "When they say it ain't the price, it's the price."

> Multinationals say there's no practical way to end outsourcing. The reality is that we could end it tomorrow.

To achieve lower labor costs, the U.S. multinationals are using their corporate consultants, such as Accenture, McKinsey, and others, to dress up the language and their rationale. And the consultants are being paid handsomely to do so. But the simple truth is that our multinationals and our elected officials who support them without reservation are callously and shamelessly selling out the American worker.

Myth No. 9: Outsourcing Enlarges America's Knowledge Base and Creates More Jobs Here

John Castellani, president of the Business Roundtable, said earlier this year, "Shifting routine computer programming, back-office, and call center jobs overseas does reduce the number of American jobs in those areas, but the cost savings generates new capital to finance the remarkable ingenuity of our economic system, to create new, higher-wage jobs here in the United States." That's the world we all wish we lived in. The problem is, there is absolutely no empirical evidence or data to support the statement. In fact, jobs lost are being replaced by lower-paying jobs.

Tom Donohue, president and CEO of the largest business organization in the country, the U.S. Chamber of Commerce, says that the United States also gains technical knowledge by exporting American jobs. Now, Tom is one of the smartest and most aggressive spokespersons for any cause or group in Washington, and a likable fellow. But he's just plain wrong. Knowledge and expertise are moving from the United States to the cheap foreign labor markets along with our jobs. We're not only exporting American jobs, we're exporting our technology advantage.

Myth No. 10: We Want to See Countries Like India Prosper

I really hope that none of the people who use this argument are suggesting that we create a middle class anywhere in the world at the expense of our own. Because for those who live and work here, for those who run companies based here, their first and foremost national concern should be the welfare of their own nation. As far as I'm concerned, there's no way you can help build your neighbor's house when your own is on fire.

Certainly we must aid other countries, but that doesn't mean we need to send our jobs to them at the expense of our own prosperity. The elitist one-worlders surely won't continue to demand that we consign our workers to an ongoing labor competition with China, the Philippines, India, Haiti, and Mexico. Those who claim that we have a higher responsibility to the world economy than to American workers might consider a visit to their local unemployment office to talk with a few of the people in the lines. Our highest responsibility is to preserve the American Dream for all Americans.

Myth No. 11: U.S. Multinationals Are Outsourcing Because Americans Aren't Well Enough Educated to Fill the Jobs

First, it's simply untrue. The more jobs Corporate America outsources, the fewer workers to pay, local, state, and federal taxes, which further punishes our struggling public education system. As Corporate America is fond of saying, companies don't pay taxes; people do. And if people don't have jobs, our tax base diminishes, and we have less to support public education. U.S. multinationals should be spending money, and setting up training for public school students, and volunteering to work in our schools, rather than lamenting the poor quality of education. In fact, we all should be doing far more to improve our public schools.

But the outsourcing of American jobs is worsening our problems, not solving them. The law of supply and demand will always determine economic choices. As Corporate America recruits more labor from third world countries, it is encouraging our young people to make educational choices that may be ominous for our ability to produce and for our future prosperity.

This past year enrollments in computer engineering jobs dropped 23 percent. MIT [Massachusetts Institute of Technology], arguably one of the most prestigious schools in the world, announced that enrollment in its engineering programs has dropped 33 percent in the past two years. Chinese schools now graduate more than 350,000 engineers every year, far above the approximately 90,000 who graduate annually from American institutions.

I hear some of the world's biggest technology companies bragging about the amount of money they spend on research and development [R&D]. But they don't always make the distinction between R&D that's going on in this country and R&D that's going on in newly created facilities in other countries—facilities that house the labor that is replacing American workers. As we know, Microsoft pledged $400 million last year to create resources in India, on top of some $750 million it had already promised to China. That's more than a billion dollars that Microsoft has put into other countries while thousands of software programmers in the United States—still home to Microsoft—go looking for work.

Myth No. 12: U.S. Companies Have to Compete in a World Market

This is the fatalism defense of outsourcing. The multinationals say there's no practical way to end outsourcing. The reality is that we could end it tomorrow. Bruce Josten, executive vice president of the U.S. Chamber of Commerce, told me that the issue was complicated and that his members were still trying to figure out the ramifications, the laws, and the actual numbers of employees directly affected. I asked Bruce what he would think of a moratorium on outsourcing by Corporate America until his colleagues worked out the details with Congress and academia. Josten said he'd rather see Congress pass tort reform and rather we had a moratorium on politicians at the state level introducing bills to stop outsourcing. In other words, no moratorium on outsourcing—even though that would at least temporarily halt the practice and give us the time necessary to determine how many jobs have been shipped out of the country and how many more are at risk, and time to create a national policy on the subject. But of course, that's the real point: Corporate America doesn't want the public to know the real numbers, or the real impact, and the last thing it wants is—God forbid—a national policy on the issue.

All these myths and the facts that dispel them have been part of the early stages of a public dialogue, from the factory floor to the set of my show, from the floor of the U.S. Senate to the water cooler. Despite the extraordinary efforts of the multinationals, their lobbyists, and the politicians they support to distort the debate on the critical issue of outsourcing, I believe that nearly all working Americans understand that not only truth is being assaulted but also our economic future and our way of life.

2

Outsourcing Does Not Harm America

Tim Kane, Brett D. Schaefer, and Alison Acosta Fraser

Tim Kane is a research fellow in macroeconomics at the Center for Data Analysis; Brett D. Schaefer is a research fellow at the Center for International Trade and Economics, and Alison Acosta Fraser is director of the Thomas A. Roe Institute for Economic Policy Studies, all at the Heritage Foundation, a political research institute in Washington, D.C.

Every time there is a slight downturn in the U.S. economy, reports about the evils of outsourcing abound. However, placing the blame on outsourcing will not help the economy and could in fact cause great harm. Studies have shown that despite the myths, outsourcing has little impact on overall job turnover in the United States and that more Americans are employed today than ever before. In fact, the number of jobs lost overseas is far less than the number of jobs being created in the United States. Over time, outsourcing will lead to more efficient businesses, better jobs, higher living standards, and overall economic growth—improvements that will benefit all Americans.

The American economy never rests—at this moment, in fact, economic growth is vigorous. Yet every time there is a slight dip in the acceleration of output, jobs, or incomes, the undying myths of a sputtering, backfiring economy rise again. Today, many of those myths concern the ills of outsourcing.

The plain facts, however, lay all of today's myths about outsourcing to rest. But there is still a real danger that politicians working with incomplete or incorrect information will hobble American competitiveness. Scapegoating poor Third World countries, "Benedict Arnold CEOs," and free trade will not improve the U.S. economy or labor market, but would likely cause great harm. Robert McTeer of the Federal Reserve Bank of Dallas summed up the promise of government action on outsourcing well: "If we are lucky, we can get through the year without doing something really, really stupid."

Dangerous Myths

Myth #1: America is losing jobs.

Fact: More Americans are employed than ever before.

The household employment survey of Americans indicates that there are 1.9 million more Americans employed since the recession ended in November 2001. There are 138.3 million workers in the U.S. economy today—more than ever before.

Myth #2: The low unemployment rate excludes many discouraged workers.

Fact: Unemployment is dropping, despite a surging labor force.

Not only is the unemployment rate low in historical terms at 5.6 percent, but the workforce has been growing—there are now 2.03 million more people in the labor force than in late 2001. Without a higher rate of unemployment or a shrinking workforce, there is no evidence of growing discouragement.

Myth #3: Outsourcing will cause a net loss of 3.3 million jobs.

Fact: Outsourcing has little net impact, and represents less than 1 percent of gross job turnover.

Over the past decade, America has lost an average of 7.71 million jobs every quarter. The most alarmist prediction of jobs lost to outsourcing, by Forrester Research, estimates that 3.3 million service jobs will be outsourced between 2000 and

2015—an average of 55,000 jobs outsourced per quarter, or only 0.71 percent of all jobs lost per quarter.

Myth #4: Free trade, free labor, and free capital harm the U.S. economy.

Fact: Economic freedom is necessary for economic growth, new jobs, and higher living standards.

A study conducted for the 2004 *Index of Economic Freedom*[1] confirms a strong, positive relationship between economic freedom and per capita GDP [gross domestic product]. Countries that adopt policies antithetical to economic freedom, including trying to protect jobs of a few from outsourcing, tend to retard economic growth, which leads to fewer jobs.

Myth #5: A job outsourced is a job lost.

Fact: Outsourcing means efficiency.

Outsourcing is a means of getting more final output with lower cost inputs, which leads to lower prices for all U.S. firms and families. Lower prices lead directly to higher standards of living and more jobs in a growing economy.

Outsourcing is a means of getting more final output with lower cost inputs, which leads to lower prices for all U.S. firms and families.

Myth #6: Outsourcing is a one-way street.

Fact: Outsourcing works both ways.

The number of jobs coming from other countries to the U.S. (jobs "insourced") is growing at a faster rate than jobs lost overseas. According to the Organization for International Investment, the numbers of manufacturing jobs insourced to the United States grew by 82 percent, while the number outsourced overseas grew by only 23 percent. Moreover, these insourced jobs are often higher-paying than those outsourced.

1. An annual report that measures the level of government intervention in the economy.

Myth #7: American manufacturing jobs are moving to poor nations, especially China.

Fact: Nations are losing manufacturing jobs worldwide, even China.

America is not alone in experiencing declines in manufacturing jobs. U.S. manufacturing employment declined 11 percent between 1995 and 2002, which is identical to the average world decline. China has seen a sharper decline, losing 15 percent of its industrial jobs over the same period.

Myth #8: Only greedy corporations benefit from outsourcing.

Fact: Everyone benefits from outsourcing.

Outsourcing is about efficiency. As costs decline, every consumer benefits, including those who lose their jobs to outsourcing. A 2003 study by Michael W. Klein, Scott Schuh, and Robert K. Triest, which includes dislocation costs in its calculations, shows the benefits of trade outweighing its costs by 100 percent.

Outsourcing is about efficiency. As costs decline, every consumer benefits, including those who lose their jobs to outsourcing.

Myth #9: The government can protect American workers from outsourcing.

Fact: Protectionism is isolationism and has a history of failure.

Proposals to punish businesses that outsource jobs, institute tariffs, or change tax rules will carry unintended consequences if enacted. Such measures would injure U.S. firms that export goods and services and erode U.S. competitiveness, often in unexpected ways. Recent steel tariffs, for example, cost jobs in dozens of industries while raising prices for consumers.

Myth #10: Unemployment benefits should be extended be-yond 26 weeks.

Fact: Jobless benefits are already working.

The median duration of unemployment is now 10.9 weeks; most workers are covered by existing benefits, which last for 26 weeks. Extending today's coverage to 39 weeks would cost billions of dollars and have little impact.

The Benefits of Outsourcing Have Been Ignored

America's workers deserve a more informative, less partisan debate on outsourcing. The negative impact of outsourcing on the economy and American employment has been greatly ex-aggerated, and the benefits of outsourcing almost entirely ig-nored.

Americans Lose Their Jobs to Foreign Competitors

William F. Jasper

William F. Jasper is an investigative reporter for the New American *magazine.*

In 2002, following suit with many of its competitors, the computer company Dell began outsourcing increasingly large amounts of work in an effort to cut costs. This trend is common to many companies across the United States, as outsourcing becomes the latest cost-saving trend. As a result of this increased level of outsourcing, American workers are forced to compete for white-collar jobs with foreign workers who are willing and happy to work for much lower wages. Unable to compete, Americans are losing their jobs because they cannot survive in the United States on the low wages that people living in developing countries are able to live on.

The mood in the conference room was light and festive. It was just two weeks before Christmas 2002 and many of the 300 or so Dell employees were getting set for the holidays and year-end vacation time as they gathered at Dell's campus in Austin, Texas, for a "town hall" meeting. They were ill prepared for the message that senior vice president Jeff Clarke was about to deliver. Meetings of this sort were usually big on awards, recognition, and introductions of new products and project teams. And despite the market drubbing of tech stocks in general, Dell had posted another banner year in sales, growth, and profits. The company also benefitted from a nice cash balance, Mr. Clarke noted. Then came the bad news. The company was announcing new personnel "attrition goals" of 10 percent per year, about double the normal attrition rate. These positions would not be filled in the United States, Clarke explained. They would be filled by new hires in India, China, and other countries where Dell is shifting business.

Audible gasps came from the employee audience, a hi-tech assemblage of Dell software engineers, electrical engineers, test engineers, group managers, and administrative talent. A Dell employee who attended the meeting told *The New American*: "A definite pall came over the crowd. It did not make for a happy Christmas."

Training Our Replacements

Although Clarke's announcement came as a shock, there had been hints of an impending axe-fall. In 2000, Dell had announced the launching of its China Design Centre in the People's Republic of China (PRC). A steady trickle of Red Chinese engineers, project planners, and managers had been brought to Dell's Austin campus for training, and some U.S. Dell employees had made the trek to China for four-to-six-month stints to train Chinese personnel there. Around the Dell headquarters in Austin, employees had begun wryly referring to the "Chinese invasion" as "training our replacements." Few expected that the replacing would start so soon.

Dell's sparkling new China Design Centre in Shanghai joins similar research and design centers in China, Russia, and India built by Microsoft, Motorola, Boeing, General Electric, and other corporate titans. The hi-tech centers are a distinctly new development, in contrast to the huge number of foreign manufacturing plants—especially in Mexico and China—built by U.S. companies over the past couple of decades. These early rounds of "globalization" cost millions of U.S. jobs, but various experts assured us that this should not concern us because these were blue collar "rust belt"[1] jobs. Old technology, they claimed. Manufacturing is passé, they said. The U.S. would enter the new global economy with the new technology. Information, services, cutting-edge research and development—these would be the clean, high-paying jobs that would keep America on top.

College grads who obtained degrees in computer science and engineering are finding themselves replaced by Third World counterparts willing to work for 20–50 percent less pay.

But guess what? After years of strip-mining America's industrial base, U.S. corporate elitists and their political allies in Washington, D.C., Beijing, Mexico, Moscow, and elsewhere are now looking to dispense with upscale white collar jobs as well. College grads who obtained degrees in computer science and engineering are finding themselves replaced by Third World counterparts willing to work for 20–50 percent less pay. In corporate globalese this replacement process is euphemistically called "outsourcing." Adding insult to injury, many of the replacement foreign workers received tax-subsidized educations in U.S. universities.

According to *Business Week*:

> In a recent PowerPoint presentation, Microsoft Corp. Senior Vice-President Brian Valentine—the No. 2 exec in the company's Windows unit—urged managers to "pick something to move offshore today." In India, said the briefing, you can get "quality work at 50% to 60% of the cost. That's two heads for the price of one."

The same issue of *Business Week* offered this glib forecast:

1. Area in northeastern and midwestern United States whose economy was formerly based largely on heavy industry and manufacturing.

Now, all kinds of knowledge work can be done almost anywhere. "You will see an explosion of work going overseas," says Forrester Research Inc. analyst John C. McCarthy. He goes so far as to predict at least 3.3 million white-collar jobs and $136 billion in wages will shift from the U.S. to low-cost countries by 2015.

Our Disappearing Competitive Edge

This is a massive shift that bespeaks far more than the number of jobs and the billions of dollars on the bottom line. It concerns the critical competitive edge that the U.S. has enjoyed due to our innovation and technological leadership. That competitive edge is disappearing. It is being given away—to our competitors and even to our avowed enemies. The *Business Week* quotes above came from the magazine's extraordinary February 3rd [2003] cover story, which ran under the alarming heading, "Is Your Job Next?" This was followed by a long cover subtitle: "The next round of globalization is sending upscale jobs offshore. They include basic research, chip design, engineering—even financial analysis. Can America lose these jobs and still prosper?"

The very obvious answer to *Business Week's* question is a resounding no! These hi-tech jobs are not luxuries that we can allow to be nonchalantly discarded. They are critically important, as are many of the low-tech jobs exported to foreign lands in recent years. Manufacturing does matter. It is essential to a strong national economy, especially for a world power like the United States with sizeable defense imperatives. We will have little hope of prosperity if we allow our nation to depend on competitors or outright adversaries for basic parts, supplies, technologies, and resources. America needs a solid base of the "old," "dirty" industries of mining, metallurgy, oil, coal, timber, steel, agriculture, and manufacturing, not only for prosperity, but for survival. All of our hi-tech advantages on the virtual battlefield will quickly prove a hollow reed if we do not have the means to produce arms, munitions, equipment, transportation, food, and clothing for our forces on the real battlefield.

That competitive edge is disappearing. It is being given away—to our competitors and even to our avowed enemies.

Under the vaunted "globalization" process, some indeed are prospering and will continue to prosper. But only an elite few. America's middle class is being squeezed and is in danger of being wiped out. If the process is permitted to continue, we will be reduced to a nation of peons ruled by a political-corporate elite indistinguishable from their socialist counterparts in China. In that tragic land, the privileged ruling class, the Communist Party's nomenklatura, live in regal splendor while the toiling masses grovel in wretched servitude.

Promises of Gain

Incredibly, *Business Week* (BW) answers its own question by suggesting that the predicted hi-tech job hemorrhage—already underway—may benefit the U.S.! "By spurring economic development in nations such as India," BW avers, "U.S. companies will have bigger foreign markets for their goods and services." How so? The same promises were made regarding low-tech jobs for the "China market." But we have found after three decades of "spurring economic development" in China that the PRC allows few of our products to reach Chinese markets. Each month China erodes more of our economic infrastructure and job base with cheap goods produced by slave labor and new factories subsidized by loans, credits, and guarantees from the U.S. government, the World Bank, and the International Monetary Fund. As Dr. Roger Canfield, author of the new book *China's Trojan Horses*, told *The New American*, "Our largest export to Red China is empty cargo containers and American jobs. Beijing turns around and sends those containers back to us with slave-labor-produced goods that continuously undercut more and more American-based businesses and our nation's security. For every dollar that we make from exports to China, we spend six dollars on imports from China. China's Communist government then uses this huge cash windfall as a strategic weapon to bribe our politicians and businessmen, buy military hardware, and obtain critical technologies and long-term productive assets that will continue to widen the trade gap—while we get consumables." India is following much the same pattern.

Nevertheless, as *Business Week* notes, "Intel Inc. and Texas Instruments Inc. are furiously hiring Indian and Chinese engineers," as are many other U.S. companies. According to that magazine voice of the Establishment corporate community, this trend should not alarm us since "a case can be made that the U.S. will see a net gain from this shift—as with previous globalization waves." "In the 1990s," BW continued, "Corporate America had to import hundreds of thousands of immigrants to ease engineering shortages. Now, by sending routine service and engineering tasks to nations with a surplus of educated workers, the U.S. labor force and capital can be redeployed to higher-value industries and cutting-edge R&D [research and development]." . . .

It has become a familiar, bitter story . . . across the country, as layoffs are announced . . . and factories are closed down. The jobs often reappear at new factories in Mexico, Indonesia, India, China.

America's white collar work force is facing the same twin battering rams of imported cheap labor and exported production that have ravaged our country's blue collar work force for years. Millions of American jobs in basic resource industries as well as manufacturing, residential and commercial construction, food processing, textiles, hotel and restaurant services, landscaping, nursing, and health care have gone to alien workers (both legal and illegal) here in this country, while millions more jobs have been outsourced to foreign lands. It has become a familiar, bitter story in cities, towns, and communities across the country, as layoffs are announced, pink slips are issued, and factories are closed down. The jobs often reappear at new factories in Mexico, Indonesia, India, China, and dozens of other countries. But the jobs in those factories don't go to U.S. workers, of course. The blue collar job drain has not let up; many more companies will move off-shore in coming years, or simply sell out to foreign corporations or larger U.S. companies that have already set up operations overseas.

Unable to Compete

Bob Davis, general manager of Modern Die Systems Inc. of Elwood, Indiana, has been watching this development for years with a mixture of alarm, sadness, and disgust. "Our government has set it up so that it is unprofitable to manufacture here in the U.S." he told *The New American*. Mr. Davis noted the tremendous disincentives to production posed by taxes, regulations, employee medical insurance, and labor union obstruction—the combined effects of which are driving many businesses into the ground, or out of the country. Occupying a hi-tech niche in the tool-and-die business, Modern Die Systems has managed to keep going, but it has had to cut its work force by about half of what it was several years ago. The company used to be very busy producing stamping dies for the automotive, appliance, electrical, recreational, heating and air conditioning, and defense industries. But, as Mr. Davis noted, "Much of my business has gone to Mexico." So have many area employers.

Dan Neuendorf, the company's president, told *The New American* about an example that typifies the dire situation he and other manufacturers face. "One of our customers in Indiana asked us to give him a quote on some metal stamping dies," he said. "We quoted a price that was as low as we possibly could go and still make any profit. But they could get it for one-fifth of our price from Red China."

Our country's entire production capability will be stripped bare. . . . And with it will go all the jobs and . . . independent businesses that are the bedrock of the American middle class.

Bob Davis said, "I told the customer that there is no way that we could match that price, but that it would be unfair and immoral for me to ask free men to work for the same wages as slaves. The company's owners are patriotic, Christian men, and they agreed that since they didn't need it right away they could let us produce it as fill-in work, according to our schedule, so that we could keep the cost down." But not all stories turn out so happily. Under tremendous pressure to cut prices, thousands of businesses opt for cheaper imported labor and/or foreign production facilities. Mr. Davis lists some of the recent losses. RCA has closed or drastically reduced its plants in Bloomington, Indianapolis, and Marion, laying off thousands. Lau Corp. of Indianapolis, a heating, ventilation, and air conditioning manufacturer, is moving assembly lines to Mexico. So is Revcor, a Carpenterville, Illinois–based producer of air conditioning fans and blower wheels. Huffy Bicycle, located in Celina, Ohio, is all but out of business, thanks to pressures from China and Mexico. Then there is the recent sale of Indianapolis-based Magnequench Inc. to China, eliminating around 400 jobs. But the Magnequench deal involves far more than jobs; it involves the sale of very sophisticated technology used to produce critical parts for smart bombs.

What is especially galling to Bob Davis is that ongoing government policies favor these trends that are killing the goose that laid the golden egg. "Our country's entire production capability will be stripped bare if this continues," he says. "And with it will go all of the jobs and small and medium-sized independent businesses that are the bedrock of the American middle class."

Job Losses to Outsourcing Are Exaggerated

Mary Amiti and Shang-Jin Wei

Mary Amiti is an economist and Shang-Jin Wei is head of the Trade Unit in the research department of the International Monetary Fund, an international organization that oversees global financial systems and offers technical and financial advice.

Hundreds of articles have been published about Americans' fears of losing their jobs to outsourcing. However, the consequences of outsourcing are not widely understood and the truth about outsourcing has been buried by news stories that generate paranoia. While it is true that some jobs are lost through the process of outsourcing, the numbers are greatly exaggerated. Although the United States does outsource a large volume of business services, the amount of work outsourced accounts for only a fraction of the gross domestic product. Furthermore, outsourcing is not leading to a net job loss; job losses in one sector are actually being offset by newly created jobs in other areas.

The outsourcing of services has received a huge amount of attention in the media and political circles in recent months, largely because media reports seem to equate outsourcing with job losses. In just five months, between January and May 2004, there were 2,634 reports in U.S. newspapers on service outsourcing, mostly focusing on the fear of job losses. But outsourcing, let alone its consequences, does not appear to be widely understood. The dictionary defines it as "the procuring of services or products . . . from an outside supplier or manufacturer in order to cut costs." However, it is not clear what is meant by "outside." Some people interpret it to mean outside the firm, and others outside the country. Media and political attention seems firmly focused on international outsourcing, even though domestic outsourcing is also common. Firms based in industrial countries that outsource services have been accused of "exporting jobs" to developing countries, with call centers and computing services in India the most frequently reported examples.

Many people would argue that outsourcing has been a normal part of international trade for decades—and they would be right. The growing outsourcing of services in industrial countries is simply a reflection of the benefits from the greater division of labor and trade that have been described for manufactured goods since the time of [Scottish political economist] Adam Smith and [British political economist] David Ricardo. What is tradable depends on technology, and advances in technology (especially in information processing, communication, and transportation) are increasingly making it possible to trade services that previously were too costly to trade. Although, for a typical industrial economy, the international outsourcing of material inputs is still far greater than that of services, the current wave of anxiety is largely about services.

Many people would argue that outsourcing has been a normal part of international trade for decades.

In the past, the service sector was largely considered impervious to international competition. For example, accountants could benefit from the cheaper imported manufactured goods that open trade allowed without fear that someone abroad would take their high-paying jobs. For this reason, service sector professionals were likely to be staunch supporters of open trade. With improvements in communication technology, such as the Internet, services can cross political borders. Jobs in fields ranging from architecture to radiology consequently seem much more at risk. Although firms were able to relocate abroad in the past, they had to give something up—their closeness to important markets, for example. With the new technologies, they can retain these links while also obtaining access to cheap but well-trained labor.

As a result, there does appear to be a backslide in support for free trade policies, particularly among white-collar workers. A study conducted by the University of Maryland found that, among individuals in the United States with incomes over $100,000, those actively supporting free trade slid from 57 percent in 1999 to 28 percent in January 2004. Furthermore, there has been a push in some industrial countries—for example, the United States and Australia—to introduce legislation that would limit the outsourcing activities of firms with government contracts. Given that little empirical work has been done to distinguish facts about outsourcing from exaggerated claims, we thought it would be useful to examine the trends in outsourcing and whether it really means job losses. On the whole, welfare should improve, but in the process some groups or individuals could be made worse off. The finer the disaggregation of data in the analysis, the more likely we are to observe "winners" and "losers." Drawing on the experiences of the United States and the United Kingdom, we can say that, in the aggregate, outsourcing does not appear to be leading to net job losses—that is, jobs lost in one industry often are offset by jobs created in other growing industries.

Trade in Services

How extensive is service outsourcing? All the media hype would lead one to believe that service outsourcing is exploding. But the data reveal that, although service outsourcing has been steadily increasing globally, it is still at very low levels in industrial countries like the United States.

In its balance of payments statistics, the IMF [International Monetary Fund] reports imports of services, which include the categories that are most closely related to outsourcing—other business services and computing and information services. Other business services comprise accounting, management consulting, call centers, and other back-office operations; computing and information comprise hardware consultancy, software implementation, and data processing. According to these statistics, U.S. business service imports as a share of GDP [gross domestic product] have roughly doubled in each of the past several decades, from 0.1 percent in 1983 to 0.2 percent in 1993 and 0.4 percent in 2003. In the United Kingdom, the share is about 1 percent of GDP. India, reported to be the recipient of significant outsourcing, itself outsources a large amount of services. Its business services grew from 0.5 percent of GDP in 1983 to almost 2.5 percent of GDP in 2003.

In value terms, the United States is the largest importer of business services. But, as a proportion of GDP, trade in business services—like trade in goods—is low compared with that of the rest of the world. In smaller countries, trade generally accounts for a larger share of GDP. Among the top 10 outsourcers of business services are small developing countries, such as Angola, Republic of Congo, Mozambique, and Vanuatu. The pattern is similar for imports of computing and information services. Among the top outsourcing countries in that category are Guyana and Namibia but also small developed countries, like Belgium and Sweden. This should not be surprising since industrial countries have the capacity to produce domestically a large proportion of the services they need, whereas many of the developing countries do not have this capacity.

Trade Is a Two-Way Street

Like trade in goods, trade in services is a two-way street. In addition to being a large importer of services, the United States is also a large exporter of services. The United States has a net surplus in all services, in contrast to its goods trade, in which it has a net deficit. In fact, the United Kingdom and the United States have the largest net surpluses in business services and hence would suffer the most in terms of the forgone dollar value of such trade if other countries cut service outsourcing.

Increases in service outsourcing in U.S. manufacturing and service sectors go hand in hand with greater labor productivity.

But that is not true of all industrial countries. The data reveal no clear pattern of developing countries being net service exporters and industrial countries net service importers or vice versa. For example, in addition to the United Kingdom and the United States, India also has a net surplus in business services. Indonesia has a large net deficit in business services, but so do Germany and Ireland.

Who's trading with whom? Contrary to popular perception, most U.S. trade in services actually takes place with other industrial countries rather than with developing countries. Using statistics from the U.S. Bureau of Economic Analysis, we found that the share of imports of "private services" from developing countries to the United States is low. (The category "private services" comprises education, financial services, insurance, telecommunications, business, professional and technical services, and other services.) In 1992, only 28 percent of U.S. imports of private services came from developing countries. Although this share increased between 1992 and 2002, it still remains quite low at 32 percent; 68 percent of these service imports originate in other industrial countries. Interestingly, only a very small proportion comes from India. In 1992, imports of private services from India were only 1/2 of 1 percent of total U.S. imports of private services. In 2002, imports of private services from India to the United States increased to nearly 1 percent of total imports of these services. There was a larger increase in U.S. imports from India in business services—a subcategory of private services—which has been the focus of most of the media attention. They increased from 0.45 percent in 1992 to nearly 2 percent of total imports of business services in 2002. The largest supplier of private services to the United States is, in fact, Canada.

Similarly, the bulk of U.S. exports are destined for industrial countries. Only 39 percent of total U.S. exports of private services go to developing countries. This fraction remained relatively constant between 1992 and 2002.

U.S. and U.K. Realities

Are more jobs disappearing than are being created as a result of outsourcing? To gain some insights, we studied the effects of foreign outsourcing of services on employment and labor productivity in U.S. industries between 1992 and 2001. The sample included all manufacturing services and five service industries for a total of 100.

Our results show that increases in service outsourcing in U.S. manufacturing and services sectors go hand in hand with greater labor productivity. Why might this be? This is likely due to firms relocating their least efficient parts of production to cheaper destinations. For manufacturing firms, the largest category of outsourced services is, indeed, business services. Even if outsourcing leads to some shedding of labor, the increased efficiency could lead to higher production and an expansion of employment in other lines of work. For example, a firm might let some employees go because it imports its information technology services but then, as it becomes more efficient, it may decide to expand its research and development department, thereby creating new jobs.

When jobs in one sector are outsourced, other sectors could also be affected. As firms that outsource become more efficient, they produce more cheaply and, hence, can provide inputs to other sectors at lower prices. This, in turn, lowers other firms' costs, reducing their prices and leading to higher demand for their products. This higher demand could be met by the increased productivity of existing staff, or, if demand growth is sufficiently strong, it could lead to further job creation, which could, in principle, offset the direct job losses caused by outsourcing. Of course, there could be a change in the skill mix of jobs.

Jobs Created in Other Sectors

In the final analysis, outsourcing does not lead to net job losses. Rather, our results indicate that, when looking at finely disaggregated sectors, you find that only a small number of jobs are lost as a result of service outsourcing. For example, when disaggregating the U.S. economy to 450 industries, there is a small negative effect on employment. But aggregating up to 100 sectors, there were no job losses associated with service outsourcing. This implies that a worker could lose her job due to outsourcing but then she, or an unemployed worker, may find a job in another firm within the broader industry classification. Hence, aggregated data would indicate that there are no net job losses when there is sufficient job creation in another sector, which indeed seems to be the case.

Evidence suggests that job losses in one industry often are offset by jobs created in other growing industries.

Are these results applicable to European and other advanced economies? To answer that question, we did a case study of the United Kingdom, examining data for 78 sectors

(69 manufacturing and 9 service), between 1995 and 2001, which was the most disaggregated data available. There, too, we found no evidence to support the notion that sectors with higher growth of service outsourcing would have a slower rate of job growth. In fact, no uniform pattern emerged between service outsourcing and employment growth. For example, the "other transport equipment" sector (which includes the manufacture of bicycles and railway) had the second highest growth in employment and one of the highest growth in service outsourcing, yet the "preparation and spinning of textile fibers" sector experienced negative employment growth over the period and was ranked one of the biggest outsourcing sectors. In contrast, both the "man-made fiber" and the "machine tools" sectors experienced a large decline in employment growth, yet the "man-made fiber" sector experienced high service outsourcing growth and the "machine tools" sector experienced a rapid decline in service outsourcing.

Our results from the U.S. and U.K. studies suggest that service outsourcing not only would not induce a fall in aggregate employment but also has the potential to make firms and sectors sufficiently more efficient, leading to enough job creation in the same broadly defined sectors to offset the lost jobs due to outsourcing.

Outsourcing Does Not Equal Job Losses

Although service outsourcing is growing rapidly, it still remains a small fraction of industrial countries' GDP. And it is not dominated by lopsided, one-way outsourcing from developed to developing countries. In fact, most industrial countries do not outsource more (when adjusted for economic size) than many developing countries. The United States, for example, which is a large importer of business services, is also a large exporter of these services and, as has been noted, has a growing net surplus in business service trade.

As for fears about job loss, our studies show that jobs are not being exported, on net, from industrial countries to developing countries as a result of outsourcing. In fact, the evidence suggests that job losses in one industry often are offset by jobs created in other growing industries.

5

Outsourcing Contributes to Poverty in America

Frank LaGrotta

Frank LaGrotta has served since 1987 in the Pennsylvania State Legislature, where he is chairman of the Tourism and Recreational Development Committee.

It has been happening for many years; factories close down, operations shift overseas and hard-working Americans find themselves out of work. The U.S. government states that outsourcing is good for the economy. It admits that there are short-term pains, but offers assurances that there is nothing to worry about. This rhetoric is cold comfort for the many Americans who have actually lost their jobs to outsourcing. These people feel the pain of outsourcing in a real and frightening way. They need their jobs to feed their families, pay the rent, and take care of bills. Outsourcing may be good for the economy, but it hurts many Americans, who find themselves slipping into financial crisis.

I am talking to a man about disposable diapers, the ones babies wear. This man knows a lot about diapers, because he once worked in a diaper factory. He worked there for over a decade, until [2003] when the plant shut down and moved its operations to Mexico. He says it was something about how, all of a sudden, it became too expensive to make diapers in western Pennsylvania. I figure it was more like something about how, all of a sudden, somebody figured out how to make a hell of a lot more money making diapers in Mexico.

Frank LaGrotta, "'Outsourcing' Our Lives," *The Nation*, March 8, 2004. Copyright © 2004 by The Nation Magazine/The Nation Company, Inc. Reproduced by permission.

No Jobs

Color me cynical, but I've seen it before. The small town where I live, and that I've represented in the Pennsylvania State House for the past eighteen years, was once a center for manufacturing. In its heyday Ellwood City, which is located about thirty-five miles north of Pittsburgh, employed more than twice as many steelworkers (over 17,000 during World War II) as its present total population of 8,200.

Steel moved to Brazil, and Panama, and Korea, and. . .

We found a lamp manufacturer to move into the empty building. The new lamp-makers didn't pay as well as the old steel-makers, but 600 jobs was, well, 600 jobs. I say *was* because those lamps are now made in China.

Like I said, color me cynical, but diapers made in Mexico does not surprise me. Right now, however, the man whose life depended on those diapers is desperate. He does not want a history lesson. He wants a job, and he wants me to help him find one. I wish I could. All I can do is listen to him, as I've listened to so many others like him who come to me believing (hoping?) I can get them a job. I know that when he's finished, I will tell him I can't get him a job, even though that's not what he wants to hear. He's already been betrayed enough by his government, even though he may not know it, so the last thing I want to do is give him false hope, which means I must tell him the truth—that despite whatever he may have been told by a neighbor, or cousin, or buddy at the pool hall, there are no state highway department jobs available. In fact, there are no state jobs available in any department. I skip the part about Pennsylvania having the lowest ratio of state employees per capita in the nation and about how the recession has forced our governor, Edward Rendell, to try to reduce the payroll even more and yadda, yadda, yadda. Somehow, I doubt if knowing that would make him feel much better.

The Government's Position

[President] George W. Bush's Council of Economic Advisers released its annual report to Congress yesterday [February 9, 2004], and I am reading about it in the *Pittsburgh Post-Gazette*. When I come to the part where council chairman N. Gregory Mankiw says that "outsourcing" American jobs actually is good for the economy, I am reminded, once again, how creative the Washington wordsmiths can be (lest we forget: "Weapons of mass destruction–related program activities" [in Iraq]). I must admit that "outsourcing" is a much tidier way of describing how rich guys are shipping millions of American jobs to places where they are free to destroy the environment and disregard human rights—little-known places where they can pay human beings, some of whom hardly are old enough to go to school (assuming there is a school for them to go to), pennies a day to make things that will be shipped back to America and sold to the same people who once made the same things before the same rich guys "outsourced" their jobs.

'Outsourcing' is a much tidier way of describing how rich guys are shipping millions of American jobs to places where they are free to destroy the environment and disregard human rights.

I think about all the steel, and lamps, and diapers that were once made in western Pennsylvania. I think about the man I spoke with five days earlier. I wonder if I should call and tell him the President believes that "outsourcing" his job was "good for the economy." Maybe that would make him feel better. I decide it probably would not. I read on.

Mankiw admits there may be some short-term pain in this, but he quickly adds that Americans shouldn't worry because "outsourcing is just a new way of doing international trade. More things are tradable than were tradable in the past. And that's a good thing."

This is confusing to me. What are we trading here? As I see it, America is sending jobs to other countries. America's rich people are getting richer. America's working people are getting poorer because they are no longer working. Is it me? Am I missing something here?

I wonder if Mankiw thinks *all* Americans should not worry, or just those Americans whose jobs have not been "outsourced." Most likely the latter, I decide. I reread the statement, "more things are tradable than were tradable in the past." What "things" is he talking about? Jobs? Lives? Futures? Have these things now become "tradable" commodities, like baseball cards?

"I'll trade you four lamp-factory jobs for a spot in a diaper factory and a specialty steel-mill gig"?

I wonder if George Bush believes this. I doubt it, I tell myself. George Bush is a "compassionate conservative."

Compassion: A feeling of empathy, concern, care. . .

The Harsh Reality

Outsourcing: Treats working Americans like waste products of a Robin-Hood-in-reverse strategy to rob from the poor and give to the rich.

Outsourcing: Treats working Americans like waste products.

No, I convince myself. It can't be. A compassionate conservative—a compassionate doorknob—would not knowingly consider other people with such disdain. It is bad enough that some of these people already have no jobs; many have lost their healthcare. Some have no money to heat their home, and some have no home to heat. They've learned to stretch a dollar the way they believe politicians stretch the truth, because they don't know when—or if—they'll get another paycheck.

All they know is their kids get hungry at suppertime, and the drugstore still wants to be paid if the baby needs more medicine to make her ear stop hurting.

President Bush certainly cares about them... Right?

6

Outsourcing Raises the Standard of Living for Many Americans

James Flanigan

James Flanigan is senior economics editor for the Los Angeles Times, *where he has been a business columnist since 1983.*

Outsourcing generates huge profits for U.S. companies—in 2004 one-fourth of all American corporate profits were earned outside the United States, and it is predicted that this number will continue to rise. Although many Americans are fearful of outsourcing, there is no cause for alarm. The increased profits that companies generate as a result of outsourcing lead to higher stock prices in markets, which in turn increases the wealth of the many Americans who own mutual funds or individual retirement accounts. In addition, outsourcing improves the standard of living for billions of poor people in developing countries who are able to get jobs that were formerly unavailable.

The news from the global economy is bullish: Major U.S. corporations are reporting sharply higher earnings thanks to surging profits from overseas.

Take General Electric Co. [GE], where rising profit from foreign operations pushed overall earnings up 25% in the first quarter. And [in April 2005] Caterpillar Inc. in construction equipment, Intel Corp. in computer chips and eBay Inc., with an enormous rise in international auction trading, all reported sharply higher earnings thanks to global growth.

Indeed, a quarter of all U.S. corporate profits, or about $225 billion, were earned outside the United States [in 2004], according to the federal Bureau of Economic Analysis.

That figure seems sure to rise in coming years because developing economies, from Eastern Europe to China, are growing at about 8% a year, compared with 3% to 4% for the U.S. and scarcely any growth at all for Western Europe and Japan.

Businesspeople look at such growth in formerly poor countries and see opportunity and long-term promise.

"We are witnessing a revolution in the movement of capital," says economist John Rutledge, an advisor to President [Ronald] Reagan and the current [George W.] Bush administration.

Alarmist Outcries

Many Americans, however, look at the same emerging economies and see only a threat to U.S. jobs. Whether it's computer programming being performed in India or manufacturing of such diverse products as cars and clothing in China, the popular images of the global economy are creating anxiety at home.

This is driving political moves in Congress and alarmist outcries on television and in a rash of new books that picture U.S. workers as a vanishing species.

But the alarms get globalization all wrong.

We've been here before. In the 1960s, the anxiety was over computers idling millions of workers. In the 1980s, the rise of Japanese industry was supposed to turn Americans into hamburger flippers.

The nightmare visions didn't come true then, and they certainly won't come true today.

Computers unleashed a huge new information industry, creating many thousands of jobs. And the competition from Japan pushed America into new frontiers such as technology and healthcare, where the U.S. now dominates.

Likewise, globalization is creating wealth for American companies and new jobs at home as well as overseas.

The rise of Japanese industry was supposed to turn Americans into hamburger flippers. The nightmare visions didn't come true then and they certainly won't come true today.

A Wave of Globalization

GE is a prime example of the way the world is turning. "Globalization is an asset for us," is how GE Chairman Jeffrey Immelt puts it. He sees the developing economies of Eastern Europe, Russia, the Middle East, India and China as GE's aces in the hole.

Why? Because those countries are moving from village to city and farm to highway and therefore need GE's turbines for electric power plants, locomotives, jet airplane engines and water treatment and desalination plants.

More to the point, the GE example also demonstrates that growth abroad can lead to benefits at home. The company employs 129,000 people in the U.S., a number relatively unchanged in the last five years, and 98,000 outside the U.S., up 6% since 2000.

The non-U.S. employment seems sure to grow because foreign operations are now 49% of GE's $152 billion in annual revenue, up from 31% only three years ago [in 2002]. But work changes with technological advances, and the average job at domestic GE now pays double what it did 10 years ago, the company says. (In comparison, average weekly wages have risen only 30% over the same period, according to the Bureau of Labor Statistics.)

The truth is that modern work is increasingly shared across borders. GE, for example, makes jet engines in Evendale, Ohio, for new regional jets in China, with some parts made in China.

Servicing of GE airplane engines is performed in Prestwick, Scotland. And lease financing on airplanes is done by its U.S.-based GE Capital Aviation Services.

The company employs advanced materials and technology to make gas turbines in Greenville, S.C., for electrical plants around the world, with some parts made in other countries. "The intellectual capital components are made here," a spokesman says.

Even intellectual capital development is becoming a cross-border operation. GE in recent years has opened technology research centers in Bangalore, India; Munich, Germany; and Shanghai [China]. That means some discoveries will be coming from abroad because the U.S. certainly has no monopoly on brains. GE today has 1,800 researchers in Bangalore.

The company also has invested $100 million to rebuild the venerable research lab at Niskayuna, N.Y., where GE's early geniuses Thomas Edison and Charles Steinmetz worked in the 19th century.

Benefits for Americans

Whether the work is done in Bangalore or Niskayuna, if it makes a profit for a U.S. company it benefits Americans. As companies make more profits overseas, those earnings form the basis of higher stock prices in markets. And that expands the wealth of Americans through their pension or mutual fund or individual investment accounts.

The American economy stands to benefit mightily from rising living standards for billions of formerly poor people.

And not to be overlooked is the fact that growing profits finance expansion and new ventures everywhere for U.S. companies. GE has used its profit in recent years to expand into biotech, where it is teaming with [pharmaceutical company]

Eli Lilly & Co. for research on Alzheimer's disease, and water desalination, where it is embarking on a major contact in Qatar. It has also acquired Universal Studios [theme park], combined it with NBC [National Broadcasting Company] and is expanding both.

To be sure, the domestic jobs picture is clouded. U.S. employment growth in this economic recovery has been weaker than in previous economic cycles. And wages are not growing. A study by the Economic Policy Institute, a liberal Washington think tank, finds that productivity and profits have risen far faster than wages in the current business cycle, a reversal of the historic pattern.

Inevitably, some U.S. workers will be displaced. Management consulting firm McKinsey & Co. advocates special government and private industry insurance to finance retraining for employees.

Yes, a lot of work in the future will be done outside the U.S.—but a lot of work will be created in this country as well.

As the largest economy and the creator of most of the world's capital, the U.S. need not fear globalization. Instead, the American economy stands to benefit mightily from rising living standards for billions of formerly poor people.

7

Outsourcing Does Not Foster Free Trade

Stephen A. Marglin

Stephen A. Marglin is a professor of economics at Harvard University.

The theory of comparative advantage, first set forth by nineteenth-century economist David Ricardo, lies at the very heart of the free market system. The theory asserts that countries should specialize in areas in which they excel, or have a comparative advantage. However, despite its academic logic, the theory does not apply well to the modern world, as the example of outsourcing shows. In the current economy the majority of people work for wages and do not have an ownership stake in the company where they work. Consequently, workers often do not benefit when a company increases its profits. Large corporations may earn greater profits because of cost reductions associated with outsourcing, while workers lose their jobs. America needs to stop using outdated economic theories that are not appropriate for the contemporary world and create policies that help America and its workers.

The theory of comparative advantage claims that a country should specialize in the goods that it can produce more easily than other countries. For example, if your country is relatively better at making computer motherboards and mine is relatively better at manufacturing television sets, yours should specialize in the former and let mine do the latter.

With each country playing to its relative strengths, all would gain from trade, the theory says.

But if every country has a comparative advantage in something, why are there persistent complaints about jobs moving to Mexico, China or India?

The theory of comparative advantage was the brainchild of 19th-century economist David Ricardo, who used it to explain how Portugal and England might mutually benefit from the differences in their natural resources. Hot, sunny Portugal ought to specialize in wine, advised Ricardo. Temperate, rainy England should stick to woolen cloth.

The Problem with the Theory

But the theory doesn't apply well to the contemporary world, and outsourcing shows why.

Suppose there's an all-purpose widget that high-tech Americans can produce at several times the speed of low-tech Indians. It might seem that with all-purpose widgets, there is nothing to trade. Not so, says the economist: Even in a world of all-purpose widgets, there is a second commodity, leisure. Ricardo would say that Americans have the comparative edge in widgets and Indians enjoy the advantage in leisure, which is to say, not producing the widgets with their inferior technology. Instead, India would sell its leisure to America.

> *The theory [of comparative advantage] doesn't apply well to the contemporary world, and outsourcing shows why.*

In other words, U.S. producers should substitute Indian labor for their own. Both Americans and Indians gain from trade. We get more leisure without reducing the quantity of available widgets here because we can supplement our reduced domestic production by importing widgets made with our technology in low-wage India. In India, it's more widgets for the same amount of work, even taking account of what is shipped overseas, because a superior technology replaces an inferior one.

Where does it go wrong?

First, we don't live in Ricardo's world, where trade is determined by fixed natural resources. In his world, technology and capital are immobile: You can't move Portuguese vineyards to England, nor can England's lush sheep pastures survive in Portugal's climate. Today, technology and capital move almost as easily across international borders as within a country.

Second, the theory imagines a world of generic Englishmen and Portuguese who are both worker and consumer, both worker and owner. The Englishman raises sheep and manufactures cloth, consuming part of his production and trading the rest for Portuguese wine. A Portuguese grower-vintner produces wine for his table and ships his surplus to English tables.

Today, few of us consume a significant part of what we produce. Consumption is separate from production. Even more important, few of us own the machines, tools and equipment needed to produce goods and services. Instead, we work for wages. The distinction between worker and owner is basic to capitalism.

The American Worker Loses

The comparative advantage theory might still be useful if widget workers had a significant ownership stake in their factories, and if labor markets functioned like model competitive markets, in which workers were free to work as much or as little as they desired at the going wage. In such a world, there is, by definition, no unemployment beyond the leisure the individual chooses. Outsourcing might lower wages in this country and raise them in India, but U.S. workers would profit from the dividends and capital gains they received as shareholders, and the lower prices they paid as consumers. And these gains, according to the comparative advantage theory, would be greater than what workers lost in wages.

But American workers don't, in general, own much stock, and U.S. labor markets fall far short of the ideal in which the worker gets to choose how much to work. In today's world, we can't understand international trade in terms of abstractions like "Americans" and "Indians" because the consequences of outsourcing are dramatically different for different groups. American owners can gain while American workers lose. Consumers can gain while workers lose.

Shareholders prosper from the cost reductions associated with substituting Indian labor for American labor. Some workers lose big-time because the added leisure that comes from shifting production abroad is not widely shared. An unfortunate minority lose their jobs altogether—their "leisure" is involuntary. For these folks, the added profits generated by outsourcing are cold comfort. U.S. consumers who don't lose their jobs benefit from lower prices, again cold comfort for folks whose old jobs are now overseas.

Economists trumpet the virtues of free trade as if the differences between textbook theory and the world were of little importance.

Economists may talk about winners compensating losers, but I've never heard a convincing story about how a 50-year-old mother of two is to be compensated after her manufacturing job is outsourced. She may, if lucky, find a comparable job somewhere, but only at the price of uprooting the family. Her husband may find another job in their new place of residence. Staying put, her only alternative may be a low-paying job.

Prosperity for Some

The only clear winner would seem to be the Indian worker, who enjoys an increase in income and consumption without any corresponding increase in work time or effort. But even here the standard explanation oversimplifies: The Indians are unambiguously better off only if we don't count the costs of the disruption to their communities and other "externalities" such as the substitution of rapid Westernization for a more gradual evolution of Indian culture colliding with globalization.

Economists trumpet the virtues of free trade as if the differences between textbook theory and the world were of little importance. No wonder economics is hard to translate into a language that addresses the concerns of ordinary folks. The great 20th-century economist John Maynard Keynes began "General Theory of Employment, Interest and Money" by observing that before we can construct relevant theories for the present, we have to unlearn the useless theories of the past. In Keynes' view, shedding the old was more difficult than building the new. He concluded with the observation that "practical men" who chart national policies are more often than not the slaves of useless theories.

The practical men and women who are responsible for trade policy today are equally the slaves of outmoded dogma. The first step to a better trade policy is to clear our minds of the cobwebs of comparative advantage, the refuge of those who find it easier to justify the havoc wrought by outsourcing than to re-examine received ideas. We need trade and we need trade policy. We don't need free-market mantras.

8

Outsourcing Fosters Free Trade

Jeffrey A. Singer

Jeffrey A. Singer is a surgeon in Phoenix and an adjunct scholar with the Reason Foundation, a libertarian nonprofit think tank. He writes and lectures on regional and national public policy.

In a free market, new jobs and products are continually created while others become obsolete. In addition, more developed countries such as the United States outsource jobs that can be completed more efficiently and at lower cost in developing countries. This outsourcing has resulted in many benefits for Americans, such as increased wealth, higher living standards, and lower prices for consumer goods. Although it may be tempting to halt the spread of outsourcing in an effort to stop the initial pain from job losses, outsourcing is a natural part of the free market system from which all of society benefits. In the long run, all Americans will end up better off as free markets accelerate the economy.

The other day, while performing an emergency operation on a patient with a bleeding ulcer, it occurred to me that surgeons don't see many ulcer patients these days. Back in the 1970s and early 80s I would operate for ulcer disease every week or so. But with the advent of new anti-ulcer drugs, most ulcer surgery has been "outsourced" to non-surgical medical specialists. Surgeons have more than made up for this loss of business through the explosion in laparoscopic surgical techniques, whereby people can have gallbladder and other operations as an outpatient through small scopes passed through the navel.

Surgeons are not alone when it comes to outsourcing. In the 19th century more than 80% of American workers were agriculturally based. Technological advancements have increased American farm productivity to the point where only 2-3% of Americans work on the farm. Agricultural jobs were outsourced to developing nations as Americans moved into manufacturing, tech, and service sector jobs.

Propelling Society Forward

The last 5 decades have seen a steady outsourcing of manufacturing jobs to countries in the developing world—the US has lost less manufacturing jobs than have the rest of the economically advanced nations. In turn, the advanced nations' economies have evolved into more finance, service-sector, and high-tech-oriented industries.

Meanwhile, people in developing countries increase their wealth as they advance from poor agrarian societies to modern industrial ones. They become new consumers of technological, financial, and other services that developed countries have to offer.

Everyone in society is better off today than in the days when blacksmiths and candle makers were indispensable.

This has been the story of mankind since the beginning. Free markets provide what the great economic historian Joseph Schumpeter called a process of "creative destruction." Always dynamic, always progressive, free markets constantly generate new products, new jobs, and new wealth on the foundations of earlier creations. In the end, they replace these earlier creations. Free markets propel society forward.

Where are the blacksmiths and candle makers? Cars and light bulbs have nearly completely eliminated these jobs. But everyone in society is better off today than in the days when blacksmiths and candle makers were indispensable.

In the interest of the health and wealth of society, Americans must resist the temptation to defy the laws of economics.

Everyone Prospers

To be sure, as societies transition from one stage of economic development to another, real people feel real pain as their jobs are "creatively destroyed." But in the long run, looking at the big picture, as those whose jobs are lost find new positions in newly created fields of work, everyone prospers.

The latest example of "outsourcing" relates to low-tech jobs—mostly telephone-based tech support—being outsourced to newly emerging India, with a billion potential new customers for American products. While low-tech jobs are going to India, the Indians are performing these jobs on equipment made in the US, and their newfound wealth is being spent on US exports. Ultimately this will increase US jobs in areas where the Indians can't compete. The Americans wind up doing more of what they do best while the Indians do the same. Both societies increase their net wealth in the process. It's ultimately a "win-win."

This creative destruction phenomenon is driven, in the end, by consumers, who are always king in a free market. The consumers demand the lowest price for the best possible product. If not, they will take their business elsewhere—perhaps to foreign imports. In order to compete for the consumers' business, US companies must constantly find ways to keep costs down while keeping quality up.

All of this was originally elucidated by the great classical economist David Ricardo. He called what he discovered the Law of Comparative Advantage, a spin-off of the division of labor principle. In his day, he would have said, "If the French make better wines for less money than the English, and the English make better sweaters for less money than the French, then they both would be better off if they drank French wine and wore English sweaters."

Benefits for All

Today, ambitious political demagogues try to take advantage of the public's general lack of understanding of economic principles, as well as everyone's dismay when people are displaced by creative destruction, and they call for the government to intervene against "outsourcing." This is nothing new. They have been doing this since the days of [eighteenth-century Scottish political economist] Adam Smith.

In the interest of the health and wealth of society, Americans must resist the temptation to defy the laws of economics. They must try to understand and appreciate the benefits free markets provide to all societies.

9

Outsourcing Puts the Security of Personal Information at Risk

David Lazarus

David Lazarus is a columnist for the San Francisco Bay Area newspaper SFGate. He also appears regularly on the San Francisco television program Mornings on 2.

U.S. laws maintain strict standards to protect Americans' personal data; however, overseas outsourcing poses a new threat because these laws, made to protect Americans, are virtually unenforceable outside the United States. In a recent outsourcing scandal, a Pakistani medical transcriber threatened to post records from patients at the University of California San Francisco's Medical Center (UCSF) on the Internet. Unbeknownst to UCSF Medical Center, the medical records had made their way to Pakistan through a network of companies that outsourced the work. This incident brought to light the lack of oversight surrounding outsourcing and the security risk created when personal information leaves the country.

"Your patient records are out in the open. . . so you better track that person and make him pay my dues."

A woman in Pakistan doing cut-rate clerical work for UCSF Medical Center threatened to post patients' confidential files on the Internet unless she was paid more money. To

David Lazarus, "A Tough Lesson on Medical Privacy: Pakistani Transcriber Threatens UCSF over Back Pay," *SF Gate*, October 22, 2003, p. A1. Copyright © 2005 by the *San Francisco Chronicle*. Reproduced by permission of the Copyright Clearance Center, Inc.

show she was serious, the woman sent UCSF an e-mail earlier this month [October 2003] with actual patients' records attached.

The violation of medical privacy—apparently the first of its kind—highlights the danger of "offshoring" work that involves sensitive materials, an increasing trend among budget-conscious U.S. companies and institutions.

U.S. laws maintain strict standards to protect patients' medical data. But those laws are virtually unenforceable overseas, where much of the labor-intensive transcribing of dictated medical notes to written form is being exported.

"This was an egregious breach," said Tomi Ryba, chief operating officer of UCSF Medical Center. "We took this very, very seriously."

She stressed that the renowned San Francisco facility is not alone in facing the risk of patients' confidential information being used as leverage by unscrupulous members of the increasingly global health-care industry. "This is an issue that affects the entire industry and the entire nation," Ryba said.

Networks of Subcontractors

Nearly all [San Francisco] Bay Area hospitals contract with outside firms to handle at least a portion of their voluminous medical-transcription workload. Those firms in turn frequently subcontract with other companies.

In the case of the threat to release UCSF patient records online, a chain of three different subcontractors was used. UCSF and its original contractor, Sausalito's Transcription Stat, say they had no knowledge that the work eventually would find its way abroad.

The Pakistani woman's threat was withdrawn only after she received hundreds of dollars from another person indirectly caught up in the extortion attempt.

The $20 billion medical-transcription business handles dictation from doctors relating to all aspects of the health-care process, from routine exams to surgical procedures. Patients' full medical histories often are included in transcribed reports.

While it's impossible to know for sure how much of the work is heading overseas, the American Association for Medical Transcription, an industry group, estimates that about 10 percent of all U.S. medical transcription is being done abroad.

For two decades, UCSF has outsourced a portion of its transcription work to Transcription Stat. Kim Kaneko, the owner of the Sausalito firm, said she maintains a network of 15 subcontractors throughout the country to handle the "hundreds of files a day" received by her office.

U.S. laws maintain strict standards to protect patients' medical data. But those laws are virtually unenforceable overseas.

One of those subcontractors is a Florida woman named Sonya Newburn, whom Kaneko said she'd been using steadily for about a year and a half. Kaneko knew that Newburn herself used subcontractors but assumed that was as far as it went.

What Kaneko said she didn't know is that one of Newburn's transcribers, a Texas man named Tom Spires, had his own network of subcontractors. One of these, apparently, was a Pakistani woman named Lubna Baloch.

The Threat

On Oct. 7 [2003], UCSF officials received an e-mail from Baloch, who described herself as "a medical doctor by profession." She said Spires owed her money and had cut off all communication. Baloch demanded that UCSF find Spires and remedy the situation.

She wrote: "Your patient records are out in the open to be exposed, so you better track that person and make him pay

my dues or otherwise I will expose all the voice files and patient records of UCSF Parnassus and Mt. Zion campuses on
the Internet."

Actual files containing dictation from UCSF doctors were
attached to the e-mail. The files reportedly involved two patients.

"I can't believe this happened," Kaneko said. "We've been
working for UC for 20 years, and nothing like this has ever
happened before."

The files in question were quickly traced to Newburn, the
Florida woman, who typically handled about 30 UCSF files
every day.

An emotional Newburn said in an interview that she's as
much a victim as Kaneko. "I feel violated," she said. Nevertheless, she said she's taking responsibility for what happened,
even though she said she explicitly told Spires not to send any
work overseas. "What he did was despicable," Newburn said.

Spires could not be reached for comment. E-mail to his
company, Tutranscribe, was returned as undeliverable. . . .

---

*We don't say that outsourcing is a terrible thing. We say
that it needs to be disclosed.*

Newburn said she contacted Spires as soon as she learned
about Baloch's threat and obtained a number to reach the Pakistani transcriber at her home in Karachi. "I spoke with her,"
Newburn said. "She was very upset but said she wouldn't have
really released the files. So I said she had to take back the
threat."

Newburn agreed to pay a portion of the money Baloch
claimed she was owed—about $500—and Baloch said she
would tell UCSF that its files were safe.

On Oct. 8, UCSF received a second e-mail from Baloch. "I
verify that I do not have any intent to distribute/release any

patient health information out and I have destroyed the said information," she wrote. "I am retracting any statements made by me earlier."

A Huge Risk

The problem, however, will not go away so easily. "We do not have any evidence that the person has destroyed the files," acknowledged UCSF's Ryba.

Moreover, how can UCSF or any other medical institution prevent something like this from happening again? Should legislation be passed barring U.S. medical data from going overseas? "I don't know the answer to that," responded Amy Buckmaster, president of the American Association for Medical Transcription. "We don't say that outsourcing is a terrible thing. We say that it needs to be disclosed."

UCSF has reached the same conclusion. Ryba said the medical center is revising its contracts with transcription firms to require up-front notice of all subcontracting. At the same time, she accepts that with a growing percentage of transcription work being exported abroad, there will always be a chance that something like this could happen again.

"We'll have to live with this risk on a daily basis," Ryba said.

10

Outsourcing's Threat to the Security of Personal Information Is Exaggerated

The Economist

The Economist is a weekly news and international affairs publication of the Economist Newspaper Limited in London.

As the volume of outsourcing has grown, fears about the security of personal information have increased. Many Americans and Europeans are worried about their personal information, such as medical and financial records, being processed overseas. The reality is, however, that personal data is not at a greater risk if it is processed outside the United States and Europe in countries such as India. At ICICI OneSource, the outsourcing division of India's largest private-sector bank, for example, only two incidents of credit card abuse have occurred, involving thefts of thirty-five dollars, total. Although Americans' personal information is at risk, outsourcing is not to blame.

First they steal our jobs, then our credit-card numbers. Those seem to be the fears inspired by outsourcing back-office financial-services work to India. In both Europe and America, the argument that outsourcing costs jobs at home still has political resonance. But it is making way for another bogey: that India cannot offer the standards of privacy and data protection that consumers expect at home. Outsourcing is dangerous and perhaps even illegal. Both claims seem dubious.

They have come together in a complaint to Britain's information commissioner, the data-protection watchdog, by a customer of Lloyds TSB, a big British bank. The bank is accused of breaking the law by failing to secure its customers' explicit consent before sending personal information outside Europe.

ICICI OneSource . . . the outsourcing arm of India's largest private-sector bank . . . claims that its security standards are 'much more stringent' than those followed by firms in Europe or America.

Like many banks, Lloyds has shifted some operations to India. It has a back-office processing centre in Bangalore, and a call-centre in Mumbai. As a result, last October [2003] it announced it would be closing a call-centre in Newcastle, where 980 people were working. Lloyds insists it is "absolutely compliant" with data-protection legislation. It argues that, as the law stands, it does not need its customers' permission to export data provided it has ensured that the information is adequately protected.

Upping Security

Viewed from India, the case seems part of an ominous trend: a new front in a guerrilla campaign against the globalisation of white-collar work. Gartner, a consultancy, has forecast that security and privacy concerns will replace job losses as the top "backlash issue". Nearly 200 pieces of legislation intended to limit outsourcing are at various stages in America's Congress and most of the country's state legislatures. Dozens of them involve restrictions on the transfer of personal data.

The Indian industry is already building its defences. NASSCOM [National Association of Software and Services Companies], its national lobby, is conducting an audit of its members' security. It has also proposed a tightening of India's own information-technology act. But the top Indian firms argue that their procedures are already world-class. ICICI One-Source, for example, the outsourcing arm of India's largest private-sector bank, and Lloyds' service-provider, claims that its security standards are "much more stringent" than those followed by firms in Europe or America.

It has strenuous physical security measures protecting its computer terminals, as well as elaborate software to guard against hackers and viruses. In most cases, it says, personal data such as credit-card numbers, names and addresses do not even pass through its systems, remaining on its clients' database servers. Importantly, in an industry where job-hopping is endemic, it also says it is careful about the background checks it carries out on new employees.

Little Cause for Concern

Given the amount of outsourcing to India, there have been remarkably few security scandals. In a much-publicised case last year [2003], a woman in Pakistan, working remotely for a medical centre in California, threatened to post confidential patient records on the internet if she was not given a pay raise. (The whole point of Pakistan, of course, is that it is not India. But it is close enough to worry some.) This year [2004] Wipro Spectramind, an Indian call-centre firm, caught some of its workers making unauthorised offers in phone calls marketing services for its client, Capital One, an American financial-services firm.

> *Given the amount of outsourcing to India, there are remarkable few security scandals.*

In the areas of biggest concern to banks and their customers, however—credit-card fraud and identity theft—there have been few reported incidents, and these have been small. At ICICI OneSource, for example, Raju Bhatnagar, the chief operating officer, says that there have only been two incidents of credit-card abuse, involving the theft of, respectively, $13 and $22.

Inevitably, there will be bad news. As Simmi Singh of Cognizant, another big outsourcing firm, points out, "crime rises in proportion to volume", and this is a fast-growing industry. Moreover, even if security concerns are a cloak for protectionism, they are real enough for banks' customers. Just as many people who happily surrender a credit card to an unknown waiter are reluctant to enter its details on an encrypted website, so many will find it hard to believe that their data are no more at risk in Mumbai than in Newcastle. This is a new frontier where, as Ms Singh puts it "cyberspace meets globalisation"; and, for some people, it's pretty scary.

11

Many American Companies Need Outsourcing to Be Competitive

USA Today magazine

USA Today magazine is a monthly periodical published since 1978 by the Society for the Advancement of Education.

As the costs of starting and operating a company in the United States have increased, it has become difficult for small companies to compete in the global marketplace. As a means of survival, many small companies have looked to outsourcing as a way to cut costs and increase efficiency in their businesses. Outsourcing provides small firms with an excellent way to save money and become more profitable. The efficiency enabled by outsourcing also makes these companies more attractive to investors, thus helping them grow even more. As highly educated workers in India command much lower salaries than do U.S. workers, outsourcing has become an attractive alternative for small companies looking to get ahead. The benefits to American companies from outsourcing can be huge, but for many small companies outsourcing is simply a matter of survival.

Will the small business sector—the nation's largest creator of new jobs over the last decade—become the biggest outsourcer to foreign countries? They may be left with little choice, notes John A. Challenger, CEO of the global outplacement firm Challenger, Gray & Christmas, Inc., Chicago.

"It is a matter of survival for these firms, especially those in the information technology sector where the company's highest costs can be payroll," he explains. "One venture capitalist even told our researchers that it would be virtually impossible to start a new IT [information technology] or software company in Silicon Valley [California] without offshore outsourcing." Small business could lobby to gain an exemption from the proposed Federal legislation seeking to curb American companies from shipping work overseas.

"Small business, defined as those with 500 or fewer employees, could argue that, as they are the No. 1 creator of jobs, and as they too are competing in the global marketplace, an exemption to the proposed law would also gain domestic jobs as they out-compete foreign firms on the basis of superior American-made product quality, service, and price," Challenger suggests.

In fact, Warren Weiss, general partner at Menlo Park, Calif.–based Foundation Capital, relates, "There's no way you can have a Silicon Valley company without outsourcing. You simply cannot make the numbers work."

That sentiment was echoed by Venetia Kontogouris, managing director for Trident Capital, based in Westport, Conn., with offices in Palo Alto, Calif. "It is far too expensive today to start a technology business in Silicon Valley without outsourcing. The economies of salary simply do not make it possible. Companies can go to India and get highly skilled workers with PhDs for the equivalent of $15,000 to $20,000 per year. You can have a team of five to six programmers in India for about the same cost as having one or two in Silicon Valley."

More Profitable Companies

The need for cost containment has increased in recent years as venture capital firms become more frugal with their investment dollars. Before the dot.com collapse,[1] it was common for

1. The sudden collapse of many Internet commerce and computer industries after the speculative frenzy of investment in Internet-related enterprises during the late 1990s.

new companies to receive as much as $15,000,000 in the initial round of venture capital funding. Today, most get $3,000,000 or less for the first year, which means they only can spend about $250,000 per month.

There's no way you can have a Silicon Valley company without outsourcing. You simply cannot make the numbers work.

A cost analysis by one Silicon Valley employer, Solidcore Systems, calculated the cost of keeping one tech employee in Silicon Valley at $15,000 per month, which includes salary and benefits, hardware, software, taxes, and real estate costs. In New Delhi, India, a worker with the same skills and responsibilities costs the employer $2,500 per month. By sending 10 jobs to India, a start-up can slash $1,500,000 from its payroll.

Cost savings is not the only factor that makes offshore outsourcing so attractive, according to Kontogouris. "Offshoring is extremely valuable in terms of its ability to expedite product development, particularly in information technology and back-office software production. A company based in Palo Alto, for instance, has access to a 24-7 workforce."

Mark Heesen, president of the National Venture Capital Association, Washington, D.C., maintains that a company incorporating offshore outsourcing into its business plan inevitably is going to be more attractive to a venture capital firm, because it figures to see a faster return on its investment.

"If a company can bring its product to market faster and cheaper through outsourcing, it is naturally going to win out in the competition for limited funding dollars," adds Challenger.

Kontogouris expects that more and more investment will be directed to American firms that outsource services to Asia. Furthermore, she predicts that the next major area of investment will be in companies that plan to develop and sell products and services to the Asian markets—China and India in particular.

If a company can bring its products to market faster and cheaper through outsourcing, it is naturally going to win out the competition for limited funding dollars.

"The creation of these information technology jobs in India is forging a new consumer class, one that wants and needs all types of products, from software to kitchen appliances," says Kontogouris. "There are a lot of opportunities. The investment money is likely to flow to the companies that plan to tap these opportunities."

A Global Economy

It is only going to get easier for companies of all sizes to send business operations and functions overseas, as the cost structure of establishing and maintaining Internet connectivity between the U.S. and Asia used to be very expensive, but has fallen dramatically.

As prices drop, more companies will join the ranks of offshore outsourcers. One group estimates that the value of business process outsourcing will rise to $24,300,000,000 by 2007, up from $1,300,000,000 in 2002. By 2015, 3,400,000 white collar jobs are expected to be sent to foreign lands, contends the research firm Forrester, Inc.

As more money and jobs migrate overseas, there is increasing worry within the U.S. that jobs here are being destroyed permanently. The trend of increased outsourcing among small businesses is especially troubling since these firms, up until now, have been responsible for 73% of the job creation in this country.

"Some are attempting to slow the tide of offshore outsourcing, but to do so is futile," Challenger argues. "However, as certain kinds of jobs dry up here, there is no reason to think that our talented workforce will not redeploy its skills in new directions and endeavors. The cost savings and efficiency gains achieved through outsourcing will, in fact, free up resources that can be used for innovation and to expand other areas of business, thus creating new opportunities and jobs in America."

The cost savings and efficiency gains achieved through outsourcing will, in fact, free up resources.

Challenger advises that for such a workforce shift to be successful, an entirely new approach to education will be required—one that promotes lifelong learning with a strong emphasis on technology. "We should be developing programs that encourage companies, schools, and other government entities to offer skills training and tuition reimbursement to adults throughout their lives." Finally, he urges that education embrace the diversity that globalization will bring with it by focusing on international studies.

12

Outsourcing Does Not Make American Companies More Competitive

Hillary Rodham Clinton

Hillary Rodham Clinton is a Democratic senator from New York. The wife of former president Bill Clinton, she was the First Lady of the United States from 1993 to 2001.

Despite the fact that outsourcing is being trumpeted as the latest cost-saving mechanism in the corporate world, savings from outsourcing have been greatly exaggerated. When the total costs of moving and operating offshore are taken into account, savings that companies gain by paying lower wages to foreign workers is greatly reduced. To realize their competitive potential, American companies need to invest in areas such as innovation that will help them to maintain a competitive advantage, rather than focusing on outsourcing. Additionally, the U.S. government should support these companies' innovations through tax credits and direct investment incentives. Once American companies have accurate information about the real cost of outsourcing, they will likely keep their jobs at home.

You can't turn on the news without hearing about offshore outsourcing—the shipping of jobs overseas to take advantage of lower wages. This trend has spread widespread fear among working families around the country. Although these fears are legitimate, I believe that the savings from such out-

Hillary Rodham Clinton, "'Bestshoring' Beats Outsourcing," *The Wall Street Journal*, July 27, 2004. Copyright © 2004 by Dow Jones & Company, Inc. All rights reserved. Reproduced by permission.

sourcing are exaggerated and that America is more competitive than most realize.

Studying the Facts

That's why New Jobs for New York, a nonprofit corporation focused on economic development, commissioned a study by [professor and consultant] Howard Rubin to explore the real facts on outsourcing. He found that next year [2005], nine out of the 10 largest firms in New York are predicted to perform IT [information technology] or business-process work offshore. The primary reason given by 90% of these firms is "cost savings." So he analyzed these savings by category.

It turns out that the savings from outsourcing were not as large as many employers believe. While they cited average savings of 44% per outsourced job, Prof. Rubin demonstrates that the actual figure approximates 20%. Lower wages are only one part of the offshore equation. When you tabulate *all* the costs, our nation is more competitive than employers think.

I believe that the savings from such [offshore] outsourcing are exaggerated and that America is more competitive than most realize.

You're probably asking, "How can we compete against countries where a computer programmer's wages are $10,000 per year while the equivalent U.S. wage is $100,000?" The explanation is that additional costs must be added to the offshore wages themselves to get the complete picture on costs. Companies have to spend money for planning, offshore transition, vendor selection, technology, communications, offshore management, travel and security. Many employers do not take every one of these costs into consideration. Add up all the costs and suddenly a call-center worker with a raw wage of $5 an hour offshore has a true cost of $17. And that's why we have the potential to be competitive.

Realizing Our Potential

But to realize that potential we need a strategy that focuses on critical areas—innovation, new job creation, workforce development, connectivity expansion, and collaboration between industry, academia, labor and government. We have to equip businesses and workers to become even more competitive, further develop the digital economy, and work to end trade and tax practices which undermine competitiveness.

> *With a smarter national strategy and better information on real costs, many companies would rethink offshore sourcing.*

First, what helps us most against offshoring is our leadership in innovation. To maintain our advantage, we need a national agenda that promotes research through tax credits and further direct investments in science. We should provide new tax incentives for jobs, and eliminate perverse ones which actually reward businesses for sending jobs offshore. That's why I have co-sponsored legislation to create a 10% tax cut for manufacturers, and to close loopholes for companies that move headquarters abroad solely to avoid taxes. And [Senator] John Kerry has proposed an overhaul of the corporate tax system to eliminate the so-called deferral advantage which rewards foreign profits at the expense of domestic profits.

We also must help our workers to adapt. This means attracting more people into the science, math, engineering and tech disciplines through grants to universities and special loan programs to students. We cannot afford to fall behind India and China, who graduate far larger numbers of scientists and engineers. The Trade Adjustment Assistance Program, which provides wage assistance and retraining only to manufacturing workers who have lost jobs due to trade, should be expanded to include computer programmers, call-center workers, and other service jobs.

We also need a national broadband policy. It is inexcusable that the U.S. ranks 11th globally in broadband penetration per household. I have introduced legislation to enhance access for rural and underserved areas that would accelerate the transformation to a digital economy.

Finally, we need the kind of collaborations that have helped make India, Ireland and others magnets for offshoring. Those countries have partnerships with their businesses that help new industries get necessary support. Such programs have proven effective regionally in the U.S. and are already underway in New York through the creation of business incubators. At the national level, we should support critical new industries like alternative energy, which hold the promise of millions of new jobs.

Keeping Jobs at Home

Where do we have the talent, resources, and cost structure coming together to enable us to compete? The answer is [in] regions like upstate New York, with unmatched educational and research institutions; proximity to the financial center of the world; and a talented, educated workforce. It also has a high quality of life, and with the recent expansion of discount carriers, it's a lot cheaper to fly inside America than any flight you'd find from New York to New Delhi.

With a smarter national strategy and better information on *real* costs, many companies would rethink offshore sourcing. The choice they would make might be described as "best-shoring." It would keep more good paying jobs in America and replace the ones we have lost with even better ones.

Organizations to Contact

American Enterprise Institute
1150 Seventeenth St. NW, Washington, DC   20036
(202) 862-5800 • fax: (202) 862-7177
Web site: www.aei.org

The American Enterprise Institute for Public Policy Research is dedicated to preserving and strengthening the foundations of freedom—limited government, private enterprise, vital cultural and political institutions, and a strong foreign policy and national defense—through scholarly research, open debate, and publications. It publishes the bimonthly magazine *American Enterprise* and the *AEI Newsletter*.

American Institute for Full Employment
2636 Biehn St., Klamath Falls, OR   97601
(541) 273-6731 • fax: (541) 273-6496
Web site: www.fullemployment.org

The institute is a nonprofit organization that conducts research to develop the best means of achieving employment for all Americans able to work. It believes that full employment can be attained by unleashing the free market and minimizing or eliminating government intervention. The institute publishes the quarterly newsletter *S.T.E.P.S.* along with reports on getting people off welfare and into meaningful jobs.

Brookings Institution
1775 Massachusetts Ave. NW
   Washington, DC   20036-2188
(202) 797-6104 • fax: (202) 797-6319
e-mail: brookinfo@brook.edu
Web site: www.brook.edu

The Brookings Institution is a private, nonprofit organization that conducts research on economics, education, foreign and domestic government policy, and the social sciences. Its principal purpose is to contribute informed perspectives on the current and emerging public policy issues facing the American people. It publishes the quarterly *Brookings Review* and many books through its publishing division, the Brookings Institution Press.

Cato Institute

1000 Massachusetts Ave. NWWashington, DC   20001-5403
(202) 842-0200 • fax: (202) 842-3490
Web site: www.cato.org

The Cato Institute is a libertarian public policy research foundation dedicated to promoting traditional American principles of limited government, individual liberty, free markets, and peace. The institute explores current controversial topics such as jobs, immigration, and outsourcing. It publishes the triannual *CATO Journal*, the bimonthly newsletter *CATO Public Policy Report*, and the quarterly magazine *Regulation*.

Competitive Enterprise Institute (CEI)

1001 Connecticut Ave. NW, Suite 1250
   Washington, DC   20036
(202) 331-1010 • fax: (202) 331-0640
e-mail: info@cei.org
Web site: www.cei.org

CEI is a nonprofit public policy organization dedicated to the principles of free enterprise and limited government. It advocates the liberalization of world trade as an avenue to global prosperity. The institute believes that increasing wealth is the true key to raising labor standards. CEI's publications include the newsletter *Monthly Planet* and *On Point*.

Conference Board

845 Third Ave., New York, NY   10022-6679
(212) 759-0900 • fax: (212) 980-7014
Web site: www.conference-board.org

The Conference Board is a worldwide business membership and research network linking executives from different companies, industries, and countries with economic data, forecasts, and business analysis. Its purpose is to enhance the contribution of business to society by conducting research on a wide range of business problems. It publishes research reports on topics such as outsourcing trends, along with the monthly magazine *Across the Board.*

Council on Foreign Relations

58 E. Sixty-eighth St., New York, NY   10021
(212) 434-9400 • fax: (212) 986-2984
e-mail: communications@cfr.org
Web site: www.cfr.org

The council specializes in foreign affairs and studies the international aspects of American political and economic policies and problems. It operates a think tank that is home to some of the world's most prominent scholars. The council sponsors task forces, commissions books and reports, and publishes the journal *Foreign Affairs* five times a year. Its publications cover a wide range of issues including business, trade, labor, foreign policy, and global governance.

Economic Affairs Bureau

740 Cambridge St.
  Cambridge, MA   02141-1401
(617) 876-2434 • fax: (617) 876-0008
e-mail: dollars@dollarsandsense.org
Web site: www.dollarsandsense.org

The bureau publishes and distributes educational materials that interpret current economic information from a progressive, socialist perspective. It publishes the monthly magazine *Dollars & Sense.*

Economic Policy Institute (EPI)

1660 L St. NW, Suite 1200
  Washington, DC   20036
(202) 775-8810 • fax: (202) 775-0819
e-mail: epi@epinet.org
Web site: www.epinet.org

EPI conducts research and promotes educational programs on economic policy issues, particularly the politics of trade and globalization. It seeks to broaden the public debate about strategies to achieve a prosperous and fair economy. It publishes the quarterly *EPI Journal* and the monthly *EPI News*, which details its latest research publications.

Foundation for Economic Education
30 S. Broadway, Irvington, NY   10533
(914) 591-7230 • fax: (914) 591-8910
e-mail: freeman@fee.org
Web site: www.fee.org

The foundation publishes information and commentary in support of free markets and limited government. It frequently publishes articles on capitalism and conservatism, also covering current hot topics such as job losses and outsourcing in its monthly magazine the *Freeman.*

Heritage Foundation
214 Massachusetts Ave. NE
   Washington, DC   20002
(202) 546-4400 • fax: (202) 546-8328
Web site: www.heritage.org

The foundation is a conservative public policy research institute dedicated to the principles of free and competitive enterprise, limited government, individual liberty, and a strong national defense. It is against protectionism and advocates free trade policies. The foundation publishes the quarterly journal *Policy Review*, along with many other publications covering current topics.

Hoover Institution
Stanford University, Stanford, CA   94305
(650) 723-1754 • fax: (650) 723-1687
e-mail: horaney@hoover.stanford.edu
Web site: www.hoover.stanford.edu

The Hoover Institution is a public policy research center devoted to advanced study of politics, economics, political economy, immigration, and international affairs. It publishes the quarterly *Hoover Digest* and *Policy Review*, as well as a newsletter and special reports, including *Foreign Affairs for America in the Twenty-First Century.*

Hudson Institute
Herman Kahn Center, 5395 Emerson Way
  PO Box 26-919, Indianapolis, IN 46226
(317) 545-1000 • fax: (317) 545-1384
e-mail: johnmc@hii.hudson.org
Web site: www.hudson.org

The Hudson Institute is a public policy research center whose members are elected from academia, government, and industry. The institute promotes the power of the free market and human ingenuity to solve social, economic, and political problems. Its publications include the monthly *Outlook* and the monthly policy bulletin *Foresight.*

Reason Public Policy Institute (RPPI)
3415 S. Sepulveda Blvd., Suite 400
  Los Angeles, CA 90034
(310) 391-2245 • fax: (310) 391-4395
e-mail: feedback@reason.org
Web site: www.rppi.org

The foundation works to provide a better understanding of the intellectual basis of a free society and to develop new ideas in public policy making. It has been a leading voice in privatization and outsourcing, and in 2002 its vice president, Adrian Moore, was awarded a "World Outsourcing Achievement Award" for outstanding achievement in outsourcing research and communication. The foundation advocates individual liberty, free markets, and the rule of law. It publishes the newsletter *Privatization Watch* monthly and *Reason* magazine eleven times a year.

Urban Institute
2100 M St. NW, Washington, DC   20037
(202) 261-5244
e-mail: paffairs@ui.urban.org
Web site: www.urban.org

The Urban Institute investigates social and economic problems confronting the nation and analyzes efforts to solve these problems. In addition, it works to improve government decisions and their implementation and to increase citizen awareness about important public choices. It offers a wide variety of resources on the economy, the labor market, immigration, and international issues.

Bibliography

Books

A.T. Bell

Another Job Offshored. College Station, Texas: Virtualbookworm.com, 2005.

William
Brittain-Catlin

Offshore: The Dark Side of the Global Economy. New York: Farrar, Straus and Giroux, 2005.

Todd G. Buchholz

Bringing the Jobs Home: How the Left Created the Outsourcing Crisis—and How We Can Fix It. New York: Penguin, 2004.

Erran Carmel and
Paul Tija

Offshoring Information Technology: Sourcing and Outsourcing to a Global Workforce. New York: Cambridge University Press, 2005.

Don Corace

Offshore. Hot Springs, AR: Emerald Ink, 2005.

Paul Davies

What's This India Business? Offshoring, Outsourcing, and the Global Services Revolution. Yarmouth, ME: Intercultural Press, 2004.

Christopher M.
England

Outsourcing the American Dream: Pain and Pleasure in the Era of Downsizing. Lincoln, NE: Writers Club, 2001.

Richard L. Florida

The Flight of the Creative Class: The New Global Competition for Talent. New York: HarperBusiness, 2005.

Gene M. Grossman and Elhanan Helpman — *Outsourcing in a Global Economy.* Cambridge, MA: National Bureau of Economic Research, 2002.

Ron Hira and Anil Hira — *Outsourcing America: What's Behind Our National Crisis and How We Can Reclaim American Jobs.* New York: Amacom, 2005.

Mark Kobayashi-Hillary — *Outsourcing to India: The Offshore Advantage.* New York: Springer, 2005.

Mary C. Lacity and Leslie P. Willcocks — *Global Information Technology Outsourcing: In Search of Business Advantage.* New York: Wiley, 2001.

Jane C. Linder — *Outsourcing for Radical Change: A Bold Approach to Enterprise Transformation.* New York: Amacom, 2003.

Himadeep Muppidi — *The Politics of the Global.* Minneapolis: University of Minnesota Press, 2004.

Sundeep Sahay, Brian Nicholson, and S. Krishna — *Global IT Outsourcing: Software Development Across Borders.* New York: Cambridge University Press, 2003.

N. Sivakumar — *Debugging Indian Computer Programmers: Dude, Did I Steal Your Job?* Bridgewater, NJ: Divine Tree, 2004.

Abraham K. Turkson — *Save American Jobs: New Business Ideas to Retain Jobs in America.* Lincoln, NE: iUniverse, 2005.

Periodicals

Terry Atlas — "Bangalore's Big Dreams," *U.S. News & World Report,* May 2, 2005.

Stephen Baker and Manjeet Kripalani	"Software: Programming Jobs Are Heading Overseas by the Thousands. Is There a Way for the U.S. to Stay on Top?" *Business Week Online*, March 2004.
Frederik Balfour and Hiroko Tashiro	"Golf, Sushi—and Cheap Engineers; the Chinese Port City of Dalian Is Becoming an Outsourcing Center for Multinationals," *Business Week*, March 28, 2005.
Dina Berta	"Smaller Firms Turn to Outsourcing as Way of Managing HR, Staff's Needs," *Nation's Restaurant News*, January 10, 2005.
Mary Brandel	"BPO: Big Political Opportunity. Business Process Outsourcing Gives CIO a Chance to Lead," *Computerworld*, August 1, 2005.
David Colander	"The Long-Run Consequences of Trade and Outsourcing," *Challenge*, January/February 2005.
Geoffrey Colvin	"America Isn't Ready (Here's What to Do About It): In the Relentless, Global, Tech-driven, Cost-cutting Struggle for Business," *Fortune*, July 25, 2005.
Economist	"The Bangalore Paradox—Outsourcing and IT in India; India's IT and Outsourcing Industries," April 23, 2005.
Economist	"Time to Bring It Back Home," March 5, 2005.

Pete Engardio   "Designing Dream Machines—in India: India's Tate Consultancy and Other Outfits Are Taking On More Complex Jobs for Detroit," *Business Week*, October 17, 2005.

Tom Field   "How to Adapt Your Offshore Strategy to an Insecure World," *CIO Magazine*, January 1, 2002.

Peter Geier   "New Standing to Challenge Outsourcing," *National Law Journal*, April 25, 2005.

Sean Gregory   "Five Jobs for Our Shores: Afraid of Outsourcing? Here Are Some Growing Fields That Won't Be Farmed Out to Foreign Workers," *Time*, October 10, 2005.

Grant Gross   "Are Tech Jobs Moving Overseas?" *PC World*, July 28, 2004.

Matt Hamblen   "After the Outsourcing," *Computerworld*, November 8, 2004.

Scott C. Harris   "Outsourcing, Offshoring," *National Law Journal*, September 12, 2005.

Tom Hickey   "Outsourcing Decisions: They're Strategic," *Computerworld*, January 25, 2005.

HR Focus   "Vigilance Is Key for the Best Benefits Outsourcing Outcomes," January 2005.

A.J. Jacobs   "My Outsourced Life: Call Centers Do It. IT Firms Do It. Manufacturers

Are Doing the Hell Out of It. Even the CIA Does It. So Why Can't I?" *Esquire*, September 5, 2005.

Ken Kerschbaumer

"E! Gets Around the World: Relying on Outsourcing Lets Network Extend Reach Cheaply," *Broadcasting & Cable*, November 7, 2005.

Sean Kilcarr

"Wrenching Decisions," *American City & County*, November 1, 2004.

Erika Kinetz

"Trading Down: The U.S. Short-changes Its Outsourced Workers," *Harper's*, July 2005.

Bradley Kjell

"Computer Science Education and the Global Outsourcing of Software Production," *IEEE Technology and Society Magazine*, Fall 2005.

Leonard Klie

"Know When to Say When: Timing Is Key to Successful Outsourcing in Logistics," *Food Logistics*, April 15, 2005.

Nathan Koppel

"A Passage to India Profits," *National Law Journal*, December 6, 2004.

David L. Margulius

"The Great Business Process Hand-off—Enterprises Are Outsourcing Entire Internal Processes—and Reaping the Rewards," *InfoWorld*, May 9, 2005.

David L. Margulius

"Offshore Partnerships Demand a Wide Range of Expertise—It's Sink or Swim in the Choppy Waters of Foreign Partnership Structures," *Info-World*, August 29, 2005.

John Markoff and Matt Richtell — "Profits, Not Jobs, on the Rebound in Silicon Valley," *New York Times*, July 3, 2005.

Norman Matloff — "Globalization and the American IT Worker," *Communications of the ACM*, November 2004.

Gail McGovern and John Quelch — "Outsourcing Marketing," *Harvard Business Review*, March 2005.

Robyn Meredith — "The Next Wave of Offshoring," *Far Eastern Economic Review*, March 2005.

Michael J. Miller — "The Benefits of Offshore Outsourcing," *PC Magazine*, April 28, 2004.

Richard McGill Murphy — "Pulling the Plug: Before You Move Part of Your Business to Bangalore, Know This: It May Not Be Worth It," *Fortune*, August 8, 2008.

Nitin Nohria — "Feed R&D—or Farm It Out?" *Harvard Business Review*, July/August 2005.

Stephanie Overby — "Outsourcing's Image Problem," *Info World*, November 1, 2005.

Bart Perkins — "Don't Outsource These!" *Computerworld*, December 13, 2004.

Gareth Price and Louis Turner — "Giant Steps in Asia: Outsourcing: China and India," *World Today*, January 2005.

Saritha Rai — "A Tutor Half a World Away, but as Close as a Keyboard," *New York Times*, September 7, 2005.

John Ribeiro	"Terrorists Targeted India's Outsourcing Industry," *PC World*, August 3, 2005.
Debra K. Rubin	"Engineers See Better Times but Business Risks Still Loom," *ENR*, November 1, 2004.
Ephraim Schwartz	"BPO Battle Heats Up—Microsoft Eyes BPO Takeover, Homing in on Targeted Niche Solutions," *InfoWorld*, February 28, 2005.
Bill Schweber	"Are We Losing Our Innovation Religion? Outsourcing Innovation Starts a Dangerous Downward Spiral," *EDN*, July 7, 2005.
Tim Shorrock	"The Spy Who Billed Me: In the Post-9/11 Rush to Beef Up Intelligence, the Government Has Outsourced Everything from Spy Satellites to Covert Operations—and Well-Connected Companies Are Cashing In," *Mother Jones*, January/February 2005.
Vanessa St. Gerard	"Some States Choosing Against Outsourcing," *Corrections Today*, February 2005.
Don Tennant	"Courting Controversy," *Computerworld*, May 9, 2005.
Anthony Ting	"Outsourcing in China: Why Would You Do It? How Would You Do It?" *Industrial Engineer*, December 2004.

Reed Tucker	"Will a Floating Tech Factory Fly?" *Fortune*, September 5, 2005.
Eric Walden and James Wetherbe	"Give a Little, Get a Little," *Harvard Business Review*, September 2005.
Nick Wreden	"Bigger than Outsourcing," *Computer World*, September 27, 2004.

Index